Don't Tell Me to Relax!

Advance Praise

"So much of this book spoke to me—I could relate to every chapter and it opened my eyes to things I didn't realize I was doing to myself. One of the concepts that really resonated with me was in Chapter 6 about being addicted to the struggle. "It was an addiction and a distraction from my emotions." Sometimes I think I make myself so busy so that I don't have to think about how nervous I am about something, or how upset I am about something. I don't have time for my feelings and then all of a sudden they come pouring out of me and I feel like a crazy person! This book was an eye opener on many levels. This is my life and I can control my future."

—Chelsea Renner

"I've been in your shoes—feeling confused, embarrassed and hopeless, crying at the doctor's office looking for the answers to take away the anxiety and to just make myself feel 'normal' again. Thank you for teaching me that anxiety is so much more than just a chemical imbalance, and uncovering the real cause of anxiety starts with self-awareness. You've motivated me to take back control of my life naturally, and for that I'll be forever grateful."

—Liz Parsons

"I love your truth, your heart, your purpose, and this book! So beautifully put of our life purpose and turning the emotions (anxiety) into a positive or internal guide of communication. I will definitely be starting to journal and improve my self talk. We wouldn't be friends with people who talk to us the way we talk to ourselves. Thanks for the message and I couldn't put it down. I officially read a book in one day (that doesn't happen). Much light and love!"

—Bridget Rompel

"If you do anything for yourself this year, read this book! I love her perspective on mindset shifts, lessons, success, failure and breaking the cycle! Her tips to raise your vibe, take control of your mindset, and quit being a mean girl to yourself are binge- worthy."

—Lisa Bedard

"Just finished the book! Truth! Every single word!! Your vibe attracts your tribe and does have a ripple effect throughout your whole community and beyond! Congratulations, Kelly!"

—Andrea Rule

"These days it seems like everyone we meet is struggling with some degree of anxiety. *Don't Tell Me to Relax* is the perfect mix of humor, girl talk and practical tools for getting rid of the mess that anxiety creates in our head! I couldn't put it down! It's like having her coach you from your couch! Truly, the book is awesome and I found myself reading huge chunks at a time! I love how I can go back and review the chapters as life happens and have all the tools I need right there! It's like a workbook and humorous biography all in one! Your authenticity shines through! Can't wait to share this with others! Congrats!!"

—**Stefanie Perryman**

"Beep beep… all aboard the struggle bus! It's true… I'm addicted to the struggle. It hit me like a 12 ton brick while reading. And yes, I read this in one sitting because it is the only time I had and I need to get this done! I can't wait to read it again and again to use the methods you outlined. Thanks for writing a book that I allowed me to really see myself and not feel so alone!"

—**Natalie Karius**

"Kelly is so relatable and down to earth. This book had it all…it made me laugh and also made me reflect inward on my life. Such a great read from start to finish. It provided me the tools to deal with my anxiety and stress in a healthy, productive way. No more running and hiding and playing the victim. If you're into personal development and becoming the best, healthiest version of yourself, I highly recommend this book. It won't disappoint!"

—**Alli Davis**

"The fact that this book is so relatable is the number one thing that brings me back to read more. Just like Kelly, I found myself searching for the next thing to do and totally forgot my happiness along the way. I find her story inspirational and serves as a way to create awareness in my own life. This book is one I will definitely recommend to others who are seeking change and want to see what that looks like first hand!"

—**Christina Valenzuela**

"I could not put this book down…She had me at the cover! Totally awesome, thought provoking, and unlike anything I have read before! Kelly is spot on in this book on what happened in her own life and how we can handle our own limiting beliefs, stress, feelings of worthlessness and so much more! Pure Genius. Thank You! I can't wait till the next… there has to be another one coming!"

—**Gerry Davidson**-CEO and
Real Estate Broker in Southern Illinois

"Wow this book hit me so hard in the heart! Many parts of this book were like reading my own life story! Such an amazing, relatable book that has changed my perspective on so many levels! Kelly you truly are a sistah from another Mistah!"

—**Rachel Gregg**, Pharm D

"This was a great read! I love how open, honest and real life everything about this book is! I believe the message you are getting out is so very important and hopefully it's a first step for many people to tackle that stress and anxiety that lies within! Thanks, Kelly!"

—**Samantha Parker**

Don't Tell **Me** to **Relax!**

*Decrease Anxiety
Without Lowering
Your Standards*

KELLY ROMPEL

NEW YORK

LONDON • NASHVILLE • MELBOURNE • VANCOUVER

Don't Tell Me to Relax!
Decrease Anxiety Without Lowering Your Standards

© 2020 **KELLY ROMPEL**

Published in New York, New York, by Morgan James Publishing in partnership with Difference Press. Morgan James is a trademark of Morgan James, LLC.
www.MorganJamesPublishing.com

ISBN 978-1-64279-613-1 paperback
ISBN 978-1-64279-614-8 eBook
ISBN 978-1-64279-615-5 audio
Library of Congress Control Number: 2019907380

Cover Design by:
Rachel Lopez
www.r2cdesign.com

Interior Design by:
Bonnie Bushman
The Whole Caboodle Graphic Design

Morgan James is a proud partner of Habitat for Humanity Peninsula and Greater Williamsburg. Partners in building since 2006.

Get involved today! Visit
www.MorganJamesBuilds.com

Mia, Ryann, and Lincoln, you are the reason I chase my dreams. To my husband Luke, you are the reason my dreams come true. Thank you for the never-ending inspiration, support, and love.

Table of Contents

Introduction

"So let me get this straight, Kelly; you are a wife, a mom of three kids ages four and under, a daughter, a full-time pharmacist, a holistic anxiety coach, you are taking one on one clients, leading group coaching sessions, doing a podcast, managing your rentals, selling your home and building a new house all while living in a camper... and now you're writing a book? I'm happy for you, but you need to be careful."

I make a post on social media telling everyone how excited I am to be writing a book, and *this* is how she responds? Is she doubting my capabilities? Is she insinuating that I am doing *too* much? Doesn't she know I am pursuing my dreams? Why isn't she being supportive? She should be happy for me. Is she trying to say I'm not taking care of my myself or my family? I feel my face getting hot as I comment back a long response about how she is right about me doing all those things, and how it's not easy pursuing a lifelong dream, that my family is taken care of and always comes first, and how supportive and amazing my husband is through it all. Can't she see how passionate and totally freaking capable I am? Did she just tell me I need to *relax*? Oh no she didn't. Those are fighting words right there.

I paused as the realization hit me; I am defensive and upset because…she's right. She didn't tell me to relax, she simply was stating the obvious. She was trying to remind me that I was doing enough and "be careful" really meant "don't burn yourself out and add more unnecessary stress to your life." I *do* tend to take on too much. I get so excited about accomplishing things and forget that I'm not superwoman, and I still need to find time to sleep, eat, take care of myself, *and* have fun. Some days I feel like a successful Super Mom who's perfectly capable of juggling it all, and at other times I feel like I am living in complete chaos and I can't even remember if I showered or brushed my teeth that day.

This was me. This is *still* me sometimes. Hi, I'm Kelly, a high-energy, type-A personality who loves a big nerdy paper calendar and gets off on multitasking and crossing things off my to-do list. I pride myself on being a "doer." I am driven and goal oriented and it would make me furious when someone would tell me to "just relax." I have always been and will always be a high achiever. I love that about myself.

Okay, okay, if I am being honest, sometimes I kind of hate it too. I enjoy setting goals and striving to achieve them, but over the years, I admittedly let my motivation go too far at times. I put a ton of pressure on myself to perform and achieve my goals at all costs. I am determined, stubborn, and refuse to let much stop me, but I would be lying if I said I never overcommitted myself. Sometimes, that means I haven't always been good to myself or those closest to me along the way. I sacrificed *a lot* of fun and sometimes my health, too. I was constantly go, go, go until my body made me slow down by getting physically ill, forcing me to rest. Resting made me uneasy and nervous, because work wasn't getting done. Being a go-getter also means I can be very uptight, irritable, easily overwhelmed, and panicky. Those closest to me got the privilege of dealing with my irritability when I was feeling overwhelmed or out of control.

Can you relate? I was strong willed yet had terrible boundaries and said yes to too many things. I overcommitted myself constantly and often felt resentful, overextended, and stressed out. I was constantly overthinking everything and replaying conversations in my mind. What did they think of me? I hope I didn't offend them. I hope they liked me. I wish I had said this. I shouldn't have said that. It was like constant chaos in my mind. I suppressed my feelings, I ignored all the warning signs, and eventually I spiraled out of control. Hitting rock bottom forced me to wake up. This is what high functioning anxiety looks like, but it took me years to discover it, own it, fully embrace it, and finally thrive with it. Just like so many other high achievers with high functioning anxiety, I didn't know I had anxiety. I just knew I felt more stressed, irritable, and unhappy than I wanted to be. Owning my anxiety hurt my ego at first. I had myself convinced that the label of anxiety felt weak and out of control and meant I had a problem. Having a problem meant I had something wrong with me. My way of fixing my problems has always been to do more and be more without actually fixing the real underlying issue of why I felt the way I did. I secretly loved how productive my anxiety made me, but the more unhappy and stressed I became, the more I realized how out of control I really was. My anxiety consumed me, but after years of over doing it, ignoring it, medicating, and eventually naturally controlling it, I have figured out how to use it to my advantage. I no longer see it as a weakness, but as a gift. Anxiety is my body's way of communicating to me, and once I started to actually listen instead of running from it, everything changed.

I know how much anxiety sucks and just how scary it can be. I so deeply understand the desire to want to just make it go away as soon as possible. I get how debilitating it can be at times, but I also know just how powerful it can be if you choose to use it to your advantage. Anxiety is a complex issue that can be managed naturally *if* you are willing to look past medication as the only option for dealing with it. If you have ever gone to the doctor's office and were told it's just a chemical imbalance that requires medication, you have been lied to. Anxiety is a chemical, emotional, situational, and spiritual problem. I have yet to work with a client whose anxiety was a result of just one of these causes. This book is written for the high achiever who resents their work ethic, productivity, constant busyness, and the resulting anxiety from it all. The principles in this book are used in my coaching program, *Limitless*. This program teaches you how to uncover and overcome the limits of anxiety that hold you back from living out your best life. You do not have to give up your productivity, compromise your work ethic, or lower your standards in order to manage your anxiety. You will become more self-aware of the limiting beliefs that are stealing your happiness and holding you back from greatness. Releasing these toxic thought patterns will help you bust through the emotional barriers that have created a ceiling on your potential. The steps in this book brought me the awareness that helped me to understand why I struggled with anxiety, negative thought patterns, and self-destructive behavior, and I am so thrilled to share them with you. Stay open minded. Be willing to feel emotional. Growth can be uncomfortable, but it is always worth it.

Chapter 1

Can't Stop, Won't Stop

I was crossing the finish line of my first half-marathon, and this was the moment I had been picturing and waiting for. I had been training for this race for months, and I finally did it! I had visualized how this moment would play out countless times in my head while I was training. I would cross the finish line with a big smile on my face as I caught a glimpse of all my friends and family jumping up and down, cheering me on while holding big signs that said, "Go Kelly!". They would tell me how amazing of an accomplishment running thirteen point one miles was and how proud they were of me.

Well…that's not exactly how my big moment went down. As I crossed the finish line, it only took a couple minutes for me to go from excited, proud, and completely in shock that I actually did it, to becoming completely consumed with anxiety. I just ran an entire thirteen point one miles without puking, pooping, or passing out…so why did this feel so anticlimactic? My leg cramps hadn't even set in yet when it hit me like a ton of bricks. I had spent months training for this, and it kept me busy. Even though I actually hated running, somehow a half marathon made it on my list of things to accomplish. I was terrible at it, didn't find it enjoyable one ounce, but it kept my mind busy. If I ran too fast, I would vomit, and if I didn't concentrate when my legs would get tired, I would trip over my own two feet. I was a mediocre jogger at best, but to me that totally counted as running. I must have asked myself 1,000 times during training why on earth I even signed up for this torture. But I wasn't going to *not* do it. I mean, duh, I had already told people I would, so that meant if I didn't, people might see me as a failure. I don't back out of hard things…ever. This was the mental game I played with myself constantly. Set a goal, achieve it, on to the next goal. I never sat in the proud feeling of accomplishment for too long. This race didn't feel big enough, and I immediately started considering a full marathon. Whoa, Kelly. Slow down. That sounds like a nightmare. I just crossed the finish line and I was literally still panting. Why didn't I feel proud and excited? The anxiety crept in…and it hit me. Training kept my mind occupied and focused on a goal, and without it, I was bored and anxious. I was already contemplating my next big goal before I could even be proud of myself for what I had just accomplished. That day at the race made me take a hard look at myself. What exactly was I running from? Why couldn't I just relax? For as long as I could remember, I felt on edge, nervous, stressed, and always working towards something big and challenging. Even from a young age.

I started dancing when I was four and competitively dancing when I was eight. Dance competitions made me so nervous that I remember hiding my dry heaving back stage before and after performances. There was no better feeling than getting off that stage and getting acknowledgement from my dance teacher and parents that I performed well. High school dance competitions were no different. I would spend hours practicing even outside of the normal dance practice. I couldn't let my team down. I was obsessed with it. Even though I was a constant ball of nerves, I loved dancing. It brought me a sense of accomplishment when my peers told me how well I did. Their reactions were everything to me. I loved the feeling of overcoming a challenge, but mostly I lived for the praise. I felt validated and important in those moments, and it became a drug I needed in order to feel good. The nervousness I felt before performances was a combination of thrilling, exciting, and complete torture. Even though I would feel sick with anxiety at times, the quick hits of worthiness made it all worth the struggle…and the addiction continued.

After graduating high school, I went straight into pharmacy school. I didn't have a passion for medicine, but I was good at science and math. I remember my mom asking me from a young age what I was going to be when I grew up. I remember changing my answers over the years as most kids do: nurse, teacher, grocery bagger, flight attendant, veterinarian. But no matter my answer, my mom would lovingly remind me that I *would* go to college and get a good paying job. I remember hearing several times, "Remember, teachers don't make that much money…" I settled on pharmacy school because it fit the requirements that were engrained in my mind for years.

It was six long years of school, but I was guaranteed a good salary. So, I went for it. It was a challenge to say the least. I hated every second. I studied my butt off and made mediocre grades. I didn't party much, and definitely didn't get the typical college experience filled with beer bongs, parties, and a lot of bad decisions. I simply didn't have time. I felt like I was on survival mode for six years, and as a result, my health took a hit. Consistent heartburn, bronchitis, laryngitis, anxiety, and irritable bowel syndrome. I was sick often during my years in pharmacy school, but it never occurred to me that maybe it was stress-induced. But I survived and the day finally came. I did it.

I graduated six years later, and I had earned my doctorate. The feeling I had walking into my graduation ceremony was something I will never forget. Proud doesn't even come close.

I was beyond relieved. I felt like I could breathe again. I did it. The pressure was off. I was *finally* successful, I thought. My parents were happy, and I knew I became something they could be proud of. That white lab coat was such a big deal to me. At twenty-three years old, I felt like a real adult with a real important job and I was proud of my hard earned salary. That feeling only lasted a couple weeks, at best. The excitement of wearing my whitecoat wore off and my job was just... a job.

Even though I worked full time and picked up extra shifts, I was bored. I had anxiety when I wasn't working because I felt unproductive. What would I do to fill my free time? I can't just watch TV, no way. That is for lazy people. Watching TV gave me flashbacks of my mom being annoyed with my dad for watching too much TV. She was someone who filled every minute doing something. She had multiple jobs and never stopped. Her work ethic was incredible. So was my dad's, but he *did* (gasp!) watch TV sometimes to relax. Watching my mom, I had formed the belief that if I wasn't doing something, I was lazy and wasting time. I was often told that if I stayed busy, I stayed out of trouble. I knew there was some truth to this, because looking back, I was so busy doing things that I never got a chance to get into trouble or just enjoy being a stress-free kid. My time was filled with dance class multiple nights a week, competitions, and recitals. In reality, I had some downtime, but as a child, my perception made it feel so busy. Don't get me wrong,

I loved dancing. I loved competing. I was so used to the constant pressure and go, go, go that I didn't really know how to just *be*.

I don't want to sound like a bratty kid here. My parents worked hard because they wanted me to have the experiences. Dancing wasn't cheap. We travelled a lot. We lived in a nice home. I was a lucky kid. I am so beyond thankful my parents pushed me to do great things. They are the reason I am Miss Independent with an insane work ethic and an ambitious attitude. They taught me that if you want something, you earn it. For those lessons, I am forever grateful. But I would be lying if I didn't say the beliefs I formed from my childhood progressed into high functioning anxiety as an adult. I could get some serious stuff done and do it well, but upstairs I was an anxiety filled overachiever who was always striving for more and never felt good enough. It was a recipe for burnout and resentment. I was building a life based on what others were expecting from me instead of the life I wanted. I didn't have the confidence to know what I wanted until I knew I hated where I was.

So, I *literally* ran from my problems, instead of dealing with my thoughts and *life*. I had found myself at the finish line of a half-marathon, in a loveless marriage that was heading for divorce with a job as a pharmacist I didn't even like. I hated who I had become. I was all about image, success, and attention. I didn't have many real friends anymore, and I felt lost, lonely, and chaotic. Dealing with my thoughts felt terrifying and overwhelming, but I was tired of running from them. That finish line was where I finally felt ready to figure out why I worked so hard to live a life I was miserable living.

My life felt like a long road trip where I just drove ten hours in the wrong direction. I was a young married pharmacist making six figures, building my dream home, driving my awesome black Cadillac C.T.S., while owning multiple rental properties. Everything about that picture-perfect life was miserable. Doing all the things I was *supposed* to do felt forced and passionless. I felt like I was living a lie with a fake smile on my face.

My marriage was built on a foundation of success instead of love. All of our conversations revolved around success and money, and how we were a power couple who would one day make it big. We had similar life and business goals, and that is what brought us together and kept us together even though our relationship was rocky, chaotic, and filled with drunken drama. We would fight like crazy over business stuff, and it soon became clear to me that we were business partners first and married second. Our marriage was built on a vision for success, not love. We had started two businesses together in a short period of time and eventually our relationship couldn't stand the pressure of it all because we had no solid foundation to fall back on when things got tough.

Our divorce was huge wakeup call for me. I had to start asking myself some really tough questions as I started to rebuild my life. What did I want out of life? How did I want to feel in my next relationship? How did I get here? Who is Kelly at her core? What do I want to do with my life now? To be honest, I felt like a failure. For someone with high functioning anxiety, this was *the* worst feeling. What did people think of me? I thought for certain they thought I was a complete clown with a joke of a life. Failure made me feel out of control and crazy. My racing thoughts consumed me and without something to obsessively fill my time, I thought I might end up in padded room with a straight jacket on. Even after I got divorced, the cycle didn't end there, because I still wasn't ready to face my thoughts. I felt like I had no other choice in order to stay sane, so I went on to complete two more half marathons. Once I stopped running from my problems and started facing them head on is when everything changed. It was messy journey of ugly crying, anger, resentment, pure bliss, anxiety, depression, hatred, excitement, and fear. Through it all, I found myself, which eventually led to finding love again.

To this day, I still hate running.

Chapter 2

Breaking the Cycle

The day I found out I was pregnant with my first baby changed everything for me. I would rub my belly and think about this sweet soul I was about to bring into the world. I had a whole list of things in my mind that I couldn't wait to tell her. I wanted her to know she was perfect just the way she was. I wanted her to know that she could do whatever she wanted with her life as long as it made her happy and healthy. I would often think about how badly I wanted her to live a life of purpose and passion that made her feel fulfilled.

Of course, I planned on teaching her how to work hard and earn the things she wanted, but I also wanted her to know that we didn't hold certain expectations for her life. We didn't expect her to go to a certain college, achieve a degree to our liking, or earn a certain salary. She would have the freedom to determine her future without our judgement steering *all* her decisions. All these thoughts were lessons I had learned along the way, after I made the mistake of following societal norms that led to a life that felt driven by money instead of happiness. I fell into the trap of believing that in order to be someone, I needed a college degree, a high paying job, and important letters behind my name. I never once considered what it would actually *feel* like to work in that job every day. It never crossed my mind that I would have a schedule that made me miss evenings, weekends, and holidays with my family. I never once considered my happiness, only the stability and paychecks.

Don't get me wrong, I am beyond grateful for my education and pharmacy job. College forced me to work hard, believe in myself, and see my bright future even when it felt so out of reach. Looking back, I still am amazed I stayed the course through six years of pharmacy school. The test anxiety still haunts me. I'm not being dramatic, I *still* have dreams that I am about to take a test that I didn't study enough for. It definitely wasn't the typical college experience filled with parties and bad decisions. I was so stressed out and hyper-focused on studying that I couldn't relax and just have a good time. If my head wasn't buried in a book, then I felt guilty. I can't help but *still* feel like I missed out on many years of fun.

Pharmacy has connected me with the most amazing coworkers and lifelong friends and for that, I am so incredibly grateful. My job financially fueled my dream of building a holistic coaching practice based on natural ways to improve mindset. Without pharmacy, I wouldn't be able to understand and respect both the pharmaceutical and natural side of healthcare. My practice is built on a beautiful blend of both sides and, because of it, I have been able to help so many ditch their meds for a natural way to manage their mindset.

Pharmacy isn't my passion, but it certainly wasn't a mistake either. It was part of my journey and purpose. Even bigger than that, it taught me that I needed to break the cycle with my kids. It is so important to me that they know my one and only expectation I hold for them is to be truly happy and to live out a life that feels authentic and purposeful. If being a trash man or dog walker is their passion, well then, I want them to be proud of their work and do it to the best of their abilities. I am determined to make sure they know that they were enough when they were born, and that they will always be enough just as they are. So why is it so easy for me to believe they are enough no matter their success, letters behind their name, or what accolades they achieve, yet when I look in the mirror sometimes I *still* need to remind myself that I am good enough? In order to teach them self-acceptance, I was going to have to let go of the ridiculous lies and limiting beliefs I believed to be true about myself. It was time for me to take a hard look within for the sake of my family. This is where my real healing journey began.

I loved being productive and goal driven, but I hated the stress and chaos I created in my life trying to obtain something that was out of reach. I was searching for external validation when all along, what I needed was some serious self-love and acceptance. But let's be real, that doesn't *just happen*; I had to make the conscious decision to work at loving *who* I was, not *what* I did.

This book takes you through the process I created in order to help myself and my clients become the high achievers they were meant to be: highly self-aware, productive, and happy, with less stress and more confidence. Being a high achiever doesn't mean you have to be obsessed and stressed all the time. Real success happens when you are aligned with your purpose, driven by the passion to make a difference, *and* taking care of yourself. I will take you on my personal journey in hopes of helping you see yourself for who you truly are. In this book, you will learn the power of being fully aware of your thoughts. You will learn your unique suppression style and how it is hindering your emotional growth and healing. You will discover how taking the wrong kind of action is killing your productivity. Get ready to drop the perfectionism, create some healthy boundaries, and learn how to trust and co-create with the universe in order to improve productivity *and* your mood. Trust the process and commit to positive change, because the process in this book only works if you are ready and willing to. Grab your journal and some fancy gel pens, because you are going to have inspiration and emotions pouring out of you. I hope you're as excited to dig in as I am to share this with you. Let's do this.

Chapter 3

The Limit—The Achievement Trap

had this image in my mind as a young girl about what success would look like for me. I envisioned an important, high-paying job that earned me respect and a big beautiful brick home with a walk around porch on some acreage. I grew up in an upper middle-class family. My mom and dad worked hard for everything they had. In eighth grade, we moved into the "rich" neighborhood in town. It was an upper middle-class neighborhood, but it felt so high class to me. We didn't have the biggest house in the neighborhood, but I was so proud and excited to be a part of it. I always admired the houses in this neighborhood and I felt like I finally belonged. I was one of them.

I can remember visiting the house as it was being built, and how excited and proud I felt as I walked around it. One day while walking around the front yard, I saw a couple neighbor boys walking down the street towards my house. I knew them from school, and they lived in some of *the* biggest houses on the block. As they got closer, I got so excited as I was sure they were coming over to say hi and check out the house progress. As they got to the front of my house, one of the boys shouted from the street, "Hey, Kelly!" I smiled big and waved back (picture Forrest Gump waving to Lieutenant Dan on his shrimp boat). He yelled, "Your house sucks!" and kept on walking.

Huh? What? I was crushed and dumbfounded. Yeah it wasn't *the* biggest house in the neighborhood, but it was an amazing house that I was really proud of. In that moment, I created a story that my house defined my worth and that I didn't belong or wasn't worthy if my house wasn't big, beautiful, and amazing. That dream stayed alive within me and as soon as I graduated pharmacy school, I began looking for acreage to build my dream home on. Within a few years, I had built my dream house with my now ex-husband on three acres in the country. It was just as I had pictured: a big, beautiful brick ranch, complete with a walk around porch and a stocked lake. I had the house in my twenties that most don't earn until their forties. It was my trophy. I felt like I had arrived.

Just as the house was almost finished, my marriage fell apart, and I was left in that amazing home by myself. Being alone in my dream home is not something I ever thought would happen. All I ever wanted was to fill it with kids, a husband, pets, and lots of love. I remember sitting alone on my gorgeous, expensive, hand-scraped hardwood floors with my head in my hands, crying and thinking that this is not what I had planned for myself. This was *not* success. This was failure, I thought. This was me with a broken heart wishing I had never built this home. What was I thinking? What was I trying to prove? Why did I think this would make me happy? I certainly wasn't happy. I was alone and miserable in a home that was barely finished, and it felt like a huge weight to carry both financially and energetically.

In a weird way, though, the struggle and chaos was so normal to me that it became my comfort zone. Somehow, I would always find myself back in the drama of the struggle *I created* because panic and stress is what I was so used to. Overcoming something negative was, as messed up as it sounds, just another way for me to achieve. I was stuck in an ugly, vicious achievement trap. My all-time favorite thing to hear was people telling me how inspirational I was. How do you do it all? How do you keep going? Where do you find the time? I'd beam with excitement on the inside and calmly shrug and say thank you. I wore this busy badge of honor but secretly felt annoyed with people who weren't just as busy as

I was. What do they do with their time? How much TV do they watch? Must be nice. I'd rather be getting stuff done. People waste so much time. Don't they have goals? These were all conversations I had in my head.

It never occurred to me that maybe, just maybe, *I* was the one with a problem. Just because they were able to relax and enjoy their time didn't make them lazy. Just because they didn't juggle two side hustles, didn't mean they don't have goals. But I didn't see it that way at first. I hate to admit it, but I found myself secretly envious of people who weren't busy all the time. I was craving more calm and ease with my life, but had my mind made up that success required nonstop hard work and struggle. I created the chaos and had a love-hate relationship with it. I thrived under pressure, and it was motivating for me. My strong stubborn nature mixed with my insecurities made reaching goals nonnegotiable. My goals were a challenge I couldn't wait to overcome, but it was all for the wrong reasons. There is a whole different energy behind achieving when you have a passion driving you instead of a need for approval. I was thirsty for attention. It wasn't cute.

Just like anything in life, you don't know what you don't know. I had no self-awareness, and I couldn't see my own issues. Because I wasn't aware of them, I couldn't own them and fix them. My rock bottom moment of hating my life and being mad at myself is what started my personal development journey. When I discovered self-help books and personal development gurus online, oh my goodness I was like an addict who would isolate myself, hide out, and binge out on it behind closed doors. One of the most impactful things I learned was the connection between the limiting beliefs we have as adults that form from the beliefs we develop from our childhood experiences.

It was through journaling one day that I discovered my achievement trap problem. In the process of trying to uncover my limiting beliefs that were holding me back, I created a timeline in my journal and listed all the major life events that stood out in my mind. As I started from birth and worked my way to the present, I noticed a trend in my significant events. They were all times I accomplished a major achievement. The time I won first place at a dance competition. The time I was elected for student council. When we won the state competition for dance team. When I became captain of the dance team. When I got accepted to pharmacy school. When I moved out on my own. When I graduated pharmacy school. When I passed my board exams. When I bought my first nice car. When I got married and built my home. Why weren't there any normal fun life memories on my timeline, and why didn't I see them as significant? Vacations? Girl scout camp? Boating? Turning sixteen and being able to drive? My twenty-first birthday? When I got my first dog? Those were amazing memories too, but somehow they didn't make it onto my "significant" life event timeline. Why was it always achievements?

It hit me. Those moments made me feel most significant. My successes defined my worth. I know now this is wrong and ridiculous, but it had been my belief for so long. I will always get off on the feeling of achieving something. Whether it's crossing a simple to-do off my list or adding titles and certificates to my name, it all feels good. Today my desire to achieve comes from a place of passion and service. This book for example is my message, and I feel a deep need to share it and know it will fall into the hands of the people who need it the most. Of course, I want it to reach many and change lives, but I am coming from a place of sharing my struggles in order to serve, and therefore doesn't require validation or approval from anyone.

So how can you tell the difference? Ask yourself what your intentions are. Working on a passion project has different motivation. The energy behind it is exciting and it comes from a place of purpose and fulfillment. The energy of striving for things for acknowledgment from others feels needy, forced, and desperate. Think about that thing you are trying to accomplish right now. Is it for titles or accolades just for showing off's sake, or is it something that feels good even if nobody knew about it? Is your intention ego driven? Are you seeking validation or trying to impress others? I am not saying you are wrong for wanting to succeed and be noticed. You can be very successful, get noticed, and be a great leader while coming from a place of serving and helping versus seeking validation and proving your worth. We need strong leaders more than ever who aren't afraid to stand up for what they believe, and I hope you do just that knowing your message is valid and worthy *first*.

Ask yourself what success means to you. Whatever comes up for you, own it. This is your truth. There is no wrong answer. Success looks different for everyone. Grab your journal and try the timeline exercise for yourself. Draw a line across your journal and on the left, write the age you can remember your first significant memory and on the right, the present moment. Start on the left side and write in your most significant moments. What events stick out the most for you? What patterns do you see? Are your events mostly negative, positive, or a good mix of both? What feelings come up as you move through your timeline? What beliefs and stories have you formed because of your significant timeline events? This exercise brings awareness to your thoughts about the past events that helped shape you the most. Awareness is the first step in making change possible.

Chapter 4

The Limit—Anxiety Without Awareness

"When you know yourself, you are empowered. When you accept yourself, you are invincible."

–Tina Lifford

S elf-awareness is incredibly powerful and the first step in making positive change. Awareness allows you to see yourself for who you really are without judgement. It's about being honest with yourself, asking the tough questions, and being willing to face the answers. It took me a *long* time to own my anxiety. I thought I was just a hyper, goal-oriented girl who liked to stay way too busy. I knew what anxiety was; *I, of course,* didn't have it, but I felt it growing up in an intense household. My dad and mom were hard workers, *really* hard workers. I can remember them being stressed about potential layoffs at my dad's job. They always had a plan B. They often had multiple jobs and even owned a side business just in case. I can remember feeling their fear and worry. I can remember wondering what life would be like if my dad lost his job.

I never felt like we were financially suffering, but I always felt the stress and tension between my parents about the possibility of it. My dad was very intense when he was stressed. I often walked on eggshells around him, because he was easily frustrated and irritated. I hated when he flew off the handle. I can remember a particularly intense time when my parents were stressed out while building our home. It was taking longer than expected to build and our apartment lease was almost up. I was riding in the car with my dad, and we were on our way to check out the house progress. All of a sudden, he stomped on the car brakes in the middle of the road of our soon-to-be neighborhood. I looked up, suddenly expecting to see a deer or something crossing the road in front of us. There was no animal in the road. Just as I started to ask why we are stopped, he began screaming, pounding his fists on the steering wheel, and stomping his feet. I sat there in silence as I watched him and wondered if he was going to break the steering wheel. I didn't say a word. That thirty second outburst felt like hours to me. He was clearly just frustrated and letting out his emotions, but it terrified me. His anxiety always seemed to show up as irritability. I learned to steer clear and stay silent when things felt heavy. I feared ruffling feathers or bringing more stress into situations, so I learned to internalize my feelings.

As I grew up, I started to pick up on those habits. I didn't know how to effectively communicate or work through my own emotions, so I usually found myself feeling anxious and frustrated with no way to diffuse or work through it. Calm problem solving wasn't something I learned, but panic and intense emotional responses were.

This led to a problem that up until *this very moment* I haven't talked about at all. I was too ashamed and embarrassed and did my best to keep it hidden. I am bawling as I write this but knowing others need this message and can relate is my motivation for putting this incredibly hard thing out there.

My anxiety would manifest as irritability, overachievement…and self-harm. When anxiety would creep in, I would play with my eyelashes so much that they would fall out. Playing with them was a repetitive behavior that felt oddly soothing. I suffer from trichotillomania, an impulse control disorder that results in the urge to play with or pull out hair, and I want to *barf* just admitting it. I know how ridiculous and weird it sounds. I hid it for years.

I can remember exactly when I pulled for the first time. I was in fourth grade and my friend picked an eyelash off my face that had fallen out and told me to make a wish. Well, I guess I had a lot of wishes because I didn't want to wait to have one just randomly fall out and land on my face for someone to see and pick off. Pulling quickly became a comforting repetitive movement for me as I grew older. I did it when I felt stressed or worried. I did it in the car and when I studied. When I was tired it was especially bad. Some days were worse than others, and sometimes I didn't even realize I was doing it. I would be so mad at myself as I looked down and would see several pulled out and sitting in front of me. You freak! What is your problem? You are so stupid to do this! Why can't you just stop? You are ruining your once beautiful and full lashes! I would beat myself up about it and that would stress me out more and, you guessed it, would cause more pulling.

It was a vicious cycle that lasted years. As much as I hated wearing glasses, I liked that they helped hide my secret. Healing from my pulling problem wasn't easy. It took a lot of mindful awareness, habit breaking, and fear of being found out to make me stop. To this day, I still find myself feeling the urge when things get tough and have to remind myself that pulling won't help me solve my problem or help me work through my emotions. I never sought help for it, because I was honestly just too embarrassed. I felt weak and out of control when I did it. The last thing I wanted to do was admit to my problem or my anxiety. It was too painful, and it felt better to just hide it and suppress it. I knew that if I did see a doctor for it, I would be prescribed an antidepressant or anti-anxiety medication. I knew the only way to stop was to address the underlying anxiety, not mask it with a medication. I can still feel the pain of it as I write the words on this page, but it feels therapeutic to finally get it out. I know my vulnerability will help someone and that makes it worth it.

For so long, I thought of anxiety as panic attacks and excessive worrying. I didn't have panic attacks, and I was highly ambitious and pursued my goals in spite of my fears and doubts, so I didn't resonate with it. I admittedly saw anxiety as a weakness and something that held people back from their goals. I didn't realize that anxiety shows up differently for everyone. I never connected to the label of anxiety until I heard the term high functioning anxiety (H.F.A.). I found an article explaining H.F.A., and I was so relieved to know I wasn't alone. I resonated so deeply with the characteristics of H.F.A. I found more comfort in owning the label of H.F.A. because it felt more positive than just "anxiety," because high functioning to me meant I was still highly capable despite my anxiety. H.F.A. describes me perfectly. I was the hyper, people pleasing, overthinking, overcommitting, constantly apologizing, to-do list junkie with nervous habits, racing thoughts and terrible self-care. I feared failure and disappointing someone more than anything else. Perfectionism made me feel like I would never measure up or be good enough no matter how hard I tried. Seeking validation from others is what fueled me. While there is definitely a negative side to H.F.A., it also has its benefits. It has given me an insane work ethic and the ambition to achieve anything that's on my heart. Most importantly, it has enabled me to help countless people struggling with anxiety to make peace with their mind by managing the negative side of H.F.A. and using the positive side to their advantage. I love to think of H.F.A. as a gift we were given because we have a big life mission to carry out. We were made for more and can do anything we put our minds to and rarely give up on our goals. You can't thrive with your unique gifts unless you fully own and acknowledge them. Your self-acceptance starts with self-awareness.

Self-awareness is a practice you can improve over time. The most life-changing awareness practice for me was journaling. Through journaling, I discovered who I was and what I wanted out of life. It was my time to be real and raw and completely vulnerable without judgment. Writing was like listening to my soul speak. It was my higher self coming through with beautiful wisdom and real talk. When I first started, I didn't know what I was supposed to write. It seemed silly and a waste of time because I wasn't being intentional about it. What started as something that felt hard and forced, quickly became my therapy and a launching pad for my goals and dreams. Without journaling, I wouldn't be an author, own multiple businesses, and I definitely wouldn't be able to manage my anxiety naturally. Before I began writing daily, I didn't know how to manage my emotions or diffuse my anger. Through journaling, I discovered self-destructive patterns, limiting beliefs, emotional addictions, and unhealed wounds from my past. I picked up on my overly sensitive and dramatic tendencies and took ownership of some hard truths of where I wasn't taking full ownership of my life. I made peace with my past and visualized my future. Journaling allowed me to see myself for who I was and gave me the power to claim who I wanted to be in the future.

I know how powerful journaling is on a daily basis, but I believe it's even more important during a period of self-discovery. This is why journaling is a mandatory practice for my clients while we are working together. If you are just starting with journaling, here are some suggestions for making it a great experience that brings a beautiful awareness and positive change to your life:

1. Commit to it. Set a goal of writing several times a week, if not daily. Sometimes it helps to sit down and journal at the same time every day. This consistency creates a powerful habit.

2. Set your intention when you sit down to write. Are you writing to let out anger and process your emotions? Are you writing to set goals? Are you free writing whatever comes to mind? Maybe you are brain dumping your to-do list or random thoughts

because your mind feels full and your thoughts are chaotic and scattered.

3. You can't screw it up. There is no right or wrong way to do it. Stop judging yourself and just allow your pen to flow without overthinking it. Write whatever feels right in the moment. This is where your real thoughts and emotions come out.

4. Try free writing for channeling messages from a higher power. My favorite channeled message came through the night before I spoke at a women's leadership conference. I was filled with excitement and nervousness, so I grabbed my journal and said a quick prayer asking for guidance about what message the women at the conference needed to hear from me the most. My pen wrote feverishly as the words came to me. Once my pen finally stopped, I knew the message was complete. As I read it after I was done writing, I didn't even recognize or remember writing the words on the page. I shared that message with the women the next day, and so many of them confirmed to me that it was a beautiful message they felt was meant for them. Just ask for guidance, be open minded, and don't stop the download by judging or thinking too much. Let your pen just write until it's done.

5. Don't let fear of your own thoughts stop you. When I begin working with clients, so often they admit they

don't journal because they are afraid of their own thoughts. This fear is really just resistance to change. It is a way to suppress your thoughts so you don't have to identify what's keeping you stuck or holding you back from your greatness. Yes, vulnerability and change can be scary, but you wouldn't be reading this book if you didn't want to better your life in some way.

Meditation is another great way to improve your awareness and expand your consciousness. If meditation sounds like torture, I completely understand. As somebody with H.F.A., when I heard that meditation was good for anxiety, the thought of sitting still in silence with my racing thoughts sounded impossible and a complete waste of time. There are so many different ways to meditate: guided meditations, visualizations, yoga, breath work, kundalini, and walking meditation, just to name a few. Some ways take more practice than others. Start with a guided or walking meditation and as it becomes easier or more enjoyable, expand into something a little more challenging for you. I suggest looking up different types of guided meditations on YouTube and commit to just ten minutes to start. If this is overwhelming, try downloading an app on your phone. There are so many to choose from, but I highly suggest the app Headspace. It is great for all experience levels and having it conveniently on your phone makes it much easier to remember. Meditation improves mood and reduces anxiety when practiced consistently.

Personality tests can also be very insightful tools for understanding yourself. There are many different types of personality tests, but I personally love the enneagram test. It helps you see yourself on a more objective level. There are nine main types of personalities according to this test, but you uncover how your type typically reacts in positive situations and also how you manage stress. Seeing my personality categorized really help me to see myself from an outsider's perspective. It's no surprise that I am "the achiever" personality type. Check out www.enneagraminstitute.com for more information and to take the test.

As Jim Rohn said, "You're the average of the five people you spend the most time with." Take an inventory of the people you surround yourself with most often. This is another way to become more aware of yourself. The people you surround yourself with the most tend to be very similar to you. Like attracts like. This could be a loving wake-up call or a reminder of your awesomeness. It is very difficult to become the best version of yourself if the people closest to you don't support your positive transformation. Are the people around you holding you back and dimming your light? Taking a look at your closest friends can be a harsh reality. Be mindful of the energy you surround yourself with and ask if it is in alignment with the person you want to be.

If you only take away one thing from this book, take this: self-awareness must happen first. Nothing can change if you are not seeing yourself for who you truly are. This means accepting your past and present and owning your future. You can read all the self-help books in the world, but if you don't accept your truth you aren't fully stepping into your true potential.

Chapter 5

The Limit—I Need to Prove My Worth

"You're a Plain Jane, and that's why I'm dating you. I don't want to date someone that I have to worry about another guy trying to steal away from me," said my longtime boyfriend.

I just stared at him blankly as the words cut right through me. Of all the mean, hateful things he had said, somehow this hurt the worst. It was as if he was reaffirming my own thoughts and insecurities, and it hit me so hard. He was dating me because I was just *okay* enough to date, yet ugly enough to not have to worry about someone else wanting to date me? I never really thought of myself as pretty anyway, so I guess he had a good point.

"Makes sense," I replied.

35

What?! Why did I agree with him? What was wrong with me? I was a fragile teenager, convinced no one else would ever love me. I mean, why would they? I didn't think I was that interesting or pretty either. I wasn't the smartest, funniest, or most talented girl in school. I *was* kind of boring and plain. I was nothing special, just *okay*. I tried my best to fit in, so I never really stood out.

If I could go back and hug that seventeen-year-old girl, I would tell her how beautiful, smart, unique, incredibly talented, caring, and driven she was. I would tell her about the amazing future in front of her with an awesome husband who adored her and thought she was the furthest thing from a Plain Jane. I would squeeze her tight, look her in the eyes, and tell her to keep her head up because she will do big things one day. I would tell her to ditch that loser boyfriend because he clearly had low self-esteem and was just projecting his insecurities onto her. Unfortunately, though, I had lessons to learn, and staying with that boyfriend for way too long was just one of them. I attracted relationships that reflected my self-worth until I finally learned to love and respect myself.

That is when I met my husband Luke. He has never made me question my value. He lets me be me. He believes in me and my dreams and has never tried to dim my light for fear of me shining too bright. *That* is confidence. But he didn't show up in my life until I was ready to mirror a partner's love and belief in me. I had to learn to love and accept myself before I would find someone who did as well. Like attracts like.

Take a good hard look at your relationships. Does your significant other respect you? I am a firm believer you teach people how to treat you. Your closest relationships mirror you. Do you love, respect, and value yourself? Because I didn't feel worthy or think I was good enough, I spent years believing I was a Plain Jane and overcompensated to validate my worth. I wasn't okay with just being okay. I wanted to be loved, accepted, and respected.

One of my biggest achievements was earning my pharmacy doctorate. PharmD. behind my name felt amazing. Look at me; I had arrived! Being respected by others for what I had accomplished was the biggest reward. *This* was what success felt like, right?

Nope. That didn't last for long. The excitement quickly wore off. I needed to do more, earn more, *be* more. The insecurities were deep, and I never felt good enough. My lack mentality could be seen in my bank account as well. I reaffirmed my beliefs of unworthiness by finding ways to struggle and live paycheck to paycheck even with a six figure salary. The memories of not fitting in as a child and teenager, crappy relationships, and comparing myself to others who had "made it" all played a role in this vicious cycle. I had confirmation all around me that I *should* be doing more with my life.

My brother was huge motivation for me. Ten years older, wiser, and more established, I watched him build his empire of rental properties, multiple successful businesses, and even buying his own jet. I wanted to be just like him. He was a pilot, ultra-cool, calm, and everything he touched turned to gold in my eyes. Of course, I never looked at his struggles of getting laid off as a young pilot, or his failed business partnerships along the way. I just saw success. He was incredibly resourceful, resilient, smart, focused, and he took risks. That's what made him so successful. But instead of looking up to him and feeling motivated by success like I do now, I felt inadequate as I compared myself to him. I wanted to impress him. I wanted him to notice my work. I wanted his stamp of approval. And more than anything else, I wanted to measure up in my parents' eyes. I never felt like my achievements were as good as Eric's, and it was admittedly my own insecurities. It was a pressure I put on myself and it was coming from a place of unworthiness, and it simply wasn't true.

My brother is still insanely successful. He is a true inspiration, an amazing business man who I respect so much, but we have different goals and I am *finally* okay with that. My vision and dream is to make a difference in the world with a ripple effect of helping one person at a time who will then help another and raise the vibration of this planet. It took me years to accept my dreams as being good enough.

If you are struggling with feelings of unworthiness, you are not alone. Self-love is a lifelong journey we all struggle with. These are the mindset shifts that helped me go from feeling inadequate to knowing I have always been and will always be enough. Grab your journal and write what comes up for you as you work through these steps.

1. What *is* good enough? What does being enough actually mean for you? Are you able to define it? Does being enough have to do with your success? What does success look like in your opinion? When most people define success, they start with "Well I should be...". They have created a story of what success "should" look like. "Shoulds" are completely made up standards you hold for yourself. They aren't real. There are no rules to success. When you feel like you *should* have a certain about of money, success, achievements, what you are *actually* saying is that this is what you think other people expect from you or what you need in order to fit in. Living your life according to other people's standards will always leave you feeling unfulfilled. Stop living your life for approval from others and start living to make an impact even if the impact is just you being truly happy. Your happiness makes a huge impact on the people you come into contact with causing a beautiful high vibe ripple effect on the planet. The

world doesn't need you to achieve, the world needs you to be happy. So start by asking yourself what makes you truly happy.

2. Comparing ourselves to others is something we *all* do. We immediately judge ourselves when we see someone who is successful and looks like they have it all together. Social media is the ultimate breeding ground for comparison and unworthiness. Seeing only the highlight reel of everyone's life makes it so easy to feel less than. I have fallen victim to the comparison trap many times which has caused me to tailspin into negative thoughts that put me in a funk for days. I lose focus, clarity, and creativity. Comparing your dream to someone else's is only killing your own. Stop thinking you have to do what everyone else is doing. You are on your own path and they are on theirs. I promise their path only looks smooth and perfect because you don't see all the ups and downs and hard work that goes into creating the life they live. Your soul has a unique purpose and if you are stuck in a space of comparing yourself, you are not fully carrying out your purpose. Take a much-needed break from social media to meditate, journal and get reconnected to yourself so you can regain your clarity and focus. Remember the grass isn't always greener...

3. Focus on progress, not perfection. When you are working towards a goal, it is so easy to forget to give yourself credit for how far you have come. Stop focusing on what you're lacking and start celebrating the progress you have made to get where you are today. High achievers tend to beat themselves up for not doing enough, but they rarely celebrate the achievements they have made along the way. What's the point in striving for goals if you can't enjoy the journey to get there? If you are unhappy before you achieve, you will be unhappy after. It's not the achievement that brings happiness, it's you.

4. Embrace the present moment. The high achiever is naturally an alpha personality who wants to conquer, push, and go, go, go, but when your mindset is constantly in the future, you never allow time to reflect and respond to life. You have to be willing to give up control and the desire to always know what's coming next. This is something I still struggle with. I have to remind myself that if I am only focusing on the future, how will that make me show up in the present? I cannot be fully in the here and now if I am always worrying about the future. How do you want to show up in the world? What energy do you want to bring? What kind of leader do you want to be? What kind of example do you want to set? Are

you okay with missing out on the present moment while you are trying to control the future? This very moment is where your power lies. You can't change the past or control the future so don't miss out on the now.

My definition of success changed as soon as I started a family. My success and worthiness used to be determined by accolades and money. Now, living a life of fulfillment and carrying out my soul's work is my motivation. This isn't what we are taught by society standards, so judgement comes easily from others who don't understand this way of thinking. I am okay with doing things differently. When I broke free from playing by the rules, I finally felt free to be myself. At the end of the day, when it comes to my happiness, I have to answer to myself. Am I living the life I want? The answer is yes. Do people understand everything I do? No, and that's okay. My husband and I got a lot of weird confused looks when we decided to sell our big brick home to move on twenty-four acres and live in a camper. We wanted to start over and build a home that was less expensive and more "us." We decided on a metal Quonset hut style home with big windows so we could look out and admire the beauty of our property. This house and property symbolized freedom to us. We wanted to be surrounded by nature but with less stuff, less of a financial burden, with more memories and freedom. People thought we were insane. They couldn't look past the fact that we lived in a camper temporarily with our kids, let alone were building a home like they had never seen before. Doing things according to our definition of success feels right even if people may view it as wrong. It's not their path, it's ours. Being brave enough to live out my dreams according to my standards gives my kids permission to do the same. I want nothing more than for them to do what lights them up and to live a life built according to their own definition of success.

Nobody gets to define success for you. No one needs to give you permission to live life the way you want to. The feeling of unworthiness you are holding onto is sabotaging your success and happiness. The next time you find yourself focusing on what you are lacking, ask where the thoughts are originating from and why you are turning to these old thought patterns. Having the awareness of the thought is more important than the thought itself. It's what's underneath the thought that holds the answer to what you are really feeling. Remember, your happiness contributes to the positive vibes of this planet and that, my friend, *is and will always be* enough.

Chapter 6

The Limit—For the Love of Struggle

"I am so sick of struggling, rushing, and living in constant chaos," I cried to my husband.

I was feeling stressed, spread thin, feeling sorry for myself and struggling to keep it together emotionally. I was making six figures as a pharmacist, I had a coaching practice on the side, my husband and I owned and managed multiple rental properties, and our family was growing at a rapid rate. I felt like we were always just getting by emotionally, financially, and physically. As soon as things felt calm for five minutes, we would be blindsided by something else that would set us back emotionally and financially. I just started to expect that the bad would always show-up to ruin the good. This was my pattern for so many years. I was emotionally addicted to struggle. I struggled through honors classes in high school when I would have thrived better in regular classes. I struggled through college. I struggled with juggling both work and school. I struggled with constant drama in my relationships. I struggled with my divorce. I struggled maintaining friendships. I struggled with anxiety. It was always something, and when I overcame an obstacle or achieved a goal, I found another way to struggle. It was constant, and I created it all.

Boredom and anxiety would set in if I wasn't feeling challenged. In true Kelly fashion, I would level up my goals, which meant a higher level of discomfort, even more hard work and stress, and, you guessed it, more struggle. My beliefs around hard work, money, and success were engrained in me as a child. I learned from watching my parents that if you want something, you earn it by working hard. My parents worked their butts off, and I formed the beliefs that nice things only came from hard work. I think this is a very typical middle-class belief, you work hard, you earn, you live a good life, you teach your kids to do the same, and repeat. My parents instilled an insane work ethic in me. I wanted to be seen as a strong woman who would always rise above my setbacks and challenges. I didn't give up without a fight. My strength from my struggle somehow gave me value. My belief that I wasn't deserving of the good things in my life unless I worked really hard for them became a form of victim mentality and self-torture. I created situations in my life to reaffirm those beliefs. Finding ways to struggle and stay stuck came easily for me.

My beliefs created this vicious cycle. I created drama out of boredom. I took on more work to create more stress. I lived paycheck to paycheck. I thrived on the rush of it all. It was an addiction and a distraction from my emotions. I was choosing to be surrounded by chaos. I manipulated myself into believing that I was worthy of success because I was an overcomer. I got to the point where I was so stressed and spread thin that I was mentally and physically unhealthy, and I resented the chaos I had created. I was exhausted. I could finally see through my own drama and it was time to call myself out. I was worthy of good things regardless of how hard I worked for them. I was tired of fighting the internal battle I had created. I was making this all too hard. I didn't really need my victim story in order to be great and neither do you.

To be fully transparent, this is a belief I am still working on healing. A lifetime of owning a belief doesn't go away with the snap of a finger, but my awareness around it has helped to quickly identify when I am falling back into that habitual victim mindset that craves the pain. When I began to include this training in my coaching programs, it became one of the biggest a-ha moments and mindset shifts for my clients. I would watch their eyes light up, their shoulders relax, and their energy soften as they came to the realization that they too were choosing the struggle mindset. Accepting ownership of this can be hard though when you aren't ready to own it. Playing the victim has its benefits. It gives you the attention you crave along with the purpose, meaning, and value you think you lack without it. If staying a victim and blaming others is what you're striving for, you can put this book down now because you aren't ready to use the power within you to change your life. If you resonate with my story and just had a massive a-ha moment, you may have uncovered something within yourself you didn't see before. The shift cannot happen without the awareness. So how do you break this exhausting struggle addiction? Grab your journal and write what comes up for you as you work through the following steps.

Decide you aren't a victim. You are in charge of your mindset. Period. Until you accept ownership of your life, you will forever live in Victimland. Let's be honest, it's easier to be a victim and blame others. It's hard to take a look at your life with the realization that you created a mess that now needs to change. Change is uncomfortable and hard work. In this case, the work is learning to change your thought patterns.

Take a long hard look at your external world because it's a reflection of your internal world. Where you are in life is a direct reflection of what you believe to be true for yourself. The crappy job (you believe you aren't good enough for something better). The degrading boss or overbearing family member (you lack boundaries). The abusive, toxic relationship (you stay because you don't think you are strong enough to leave and go through life on your own). That fit body you want so badly but don't have (you don't want it enough, because you aren't willing to do what it takes to get it). It all goes back to you.

Look, I understand I am making generalizations here and that there will always be a reason why you can prove me wrong or that it's not your fault. But it is always your choice whether or not to fall victim to your circumstances. Mindful awareness is everything. Once you own your thoughts and see how they create your world, it is up to you to do something about the things you wish were different.

Rewrite your story around struggle. Journal on who you learned it from and why it's ultimately not true. These questions may help you uncover some connections. What did your parents teach you about money? Is earning money easy for you? Who did you have to be to earn your parents love? What did your parents teach you about work ethic? Did your parents struggle to make enough money? Maybe money wasn't even discussed. What expectations did your parents have for your life as an adult? Did they expect you to go to college or was graduating from high school celebrated and enough for them? Did they want you to have a certain profession or make a certain amount of money as an adult?

How would it feel to not struggle? Would you feel guilty if money and success came to you easily? Would you be resistant to a life of ease? Would you welcome calm and aligned success, or would it feel weird to have things fall into place easily?

Choose again. Choosing new thoughts is a pattern and habit you have to create with repetition. It is decision to shift your thoughts in the moment from "this is hard" to "I am choosing to make this harder than it needs to be. I choose to allow this to be easy." Use negative situations for good. Choose to see them in a positive light and rise above them by taking a step back and seeing the big picture. Ask yourself in the moment how you are making this challenge worse or even using it to your advantage or creating it to solidify your struggle story. Give yourself permission to receive the good without the bad being a necessary part of earning it. Choose to see the value in struggle and learn from it. Get off that struggle bus.

Stay on top of your emotions through journaling. You may find it difficult to see the value of journaling when you first start. The results don't happen right away, so you get discouraged and quit. It's just like going to the gym. You're not going to be ripped or twenty pounds lighter after going two times. You have to stay consistent to see change over time.

I personally love to journal now because it frees up energetic space for me and allows me to sort through my thoughts and release my emotions in a healthy way. Ladies, we can get all up in our heads and jump on the crazy train *real* fast if we aren't careful. Journaling helps me control the crazy. It is completely worth the effort, I promise. Find a way to fit it in every day, and soon it will become something that feels good to you.

Break the cycle. What do you want to teach your kids about working hard, earning money, and success? We all want to see our kids live an amazing life full of abundance, success, and happiness. I want my kids to form healthy beliefs around success and to know that they don't have to *be somebody* in order to be worthy of my love. I will teach them how to be resilient during challenging times and how to focus on the lessons in these situations instead of being a victim.

Just remember that struggling isn't serving you. It's your birthright to be great. I'm not trying to over simplify your human experience, but I *am* saying sometimes you need to take a step back and look at the big picture. Yes, life is full of lessons. Yes, there will be hard times. But your soul's purpose isn't to struggle, it's to rise above. Stop choosing the struggle and allow yourself the grace to be a work in progress. The pressure of life is enough, quit adding to it unnecessarily and remember you are in charge here. Take your power back.

Chapter 7

The Limit—Suppression

I am the first person to admit I am a freaking pro at running from and hiding my emotions. Remember my half marathon story? I *literally* run. I think it is safe to say most people suppress their emotions, but not all people realize they are doing it. Think of the last time you got really angry or stressed. How did you handle it? Did you make a stiff drink? Grab a beer? Smoke a cigarette? Get lost in a carton of Ben and Jerry's? Binge out on trashy reality TV?

I'm not judging; I am right here with you nodding my head and raising my hand. We have all done it. It is completely normal to want to run from emotions and do anything to not have to feel them. It is our way of protecting ourselves from feeling bad. In the moment, we are choosing not to deal with

53

them, but unfortunately sometimes we are forced to hide our emotions. Maybe someone pissed you off at work and all you want to do is give them a piece of your mind and the middle finger, but instead you bite your tongue so you don't get fired. Moms, how about when your kids are wearing on your nerves all day long and after hearing "Mom, Mom, Mom" 80,000 times you have to respond, "What, honey?" when you really want to say, "Shut up pleeeeaaase." I know I have silently mouthed it. No shame here. It is completely normal to want to run from our feelings, but this is especially true for something that is painful, embarrassing, or traumatizing. Of course we don't want to deal with those things! Suppressing emotions leaves them undealt with. Unprocessed emotions end up becoming emotional baggage that take up some serious mental real estate keeping you blocked, stuck, and low vibe.

Let's talk about some of the most common suppression styles we have *all* used in order to not feel.

Distraction: Channeling your energy into something else in order to distract yourself from what you're trying not to deal with. Obsessing over your to-do list, staying busy, cleaning, starting a new project, fixing someone else's problems, *anything* to keep your mind off how uncomfortable your emotions feel. Distraction makes you feel better because you are super busy and focused, but yet still completely unfulfilled. I am a master at this! High achievers tend to focus on new projects and goals instead of doing the heavy work of dealing with what's going on upstairs. It is far easier to focus on a challenge than focusing on what's bothering us.

Numbing Out: You numb out as soon as your emotions make you feel uncomfortable. The most common ways are drinking alcohol, eating, shopping, social media, TV, drugs, working, and over-exercising. This can be any type of addiction or addictive behavior that helps you cope with or not feel your true feelings. I am totally guilty of pouring a glass of wine when I am super stressed or upset. No, I am not saying you shouldn't drink or veg out and binge on *The Real Housewives* to unwind, but I am saying that if you are dealing with emotions that stem from serious anger, stress, or trauma, numbing out will not help you in the long run. Long term stress and anger can result in very serious effects on the body that can lead to inflammation, illness, and disease. Numbing out has also been known to lead to addictive patterns and behaviors as well, making it a potentially dangerous form of suppression. I see this often with clients who hold emotional anger towards a person who hurt them deeply or after a trauma they experienced. Unfortunately, it happens a lot with addicts. They live through a traumatic experience and the pain they feel is so strong that only drugs or alcohol can numb it. I believe certain anxiety medications fall in this category as well. I am not saying you shouldn't use them if you need them. Of course, they may help in the moment, but they aren't the long-term answer for most people, in my opinion. They are another form of suppression and coping.

They can be addictive, hard on your liver, and have terrible side effects. They can help you not feel as much emotion, but they can also make you feel like an overly zenned-out space cadet. Yes they have saved lives…*and* they have also killed people. You have to be an advocate for yourself and get the help you need when you need it, but I also want to challenge you to get *really* real with yourself, and know when you need help vs when it's time to deal with problems head on and fix the underlying problem. More on this to come in an upcoming chapter.

Spiritual Bypass: If you are woo-woo, this is for you. I am definitely on the woo-woo train and have to check myself with this one sometimes. Woo-woo is my way of describing someone who is into spirituality, crystals, energy work, meditation, oracle/tarot cards, the moon, horoscopes, all the hippy dippy stuff I am into. To me, my "woo-ness" is just normal. It is very common for people who are very spiritual to immediately try to bypass emotions by replacing their feelings with their spiritual beliefs. For example, when you are emotionally triggered, you may be quick to jump to the potential lessons learned, telling yourself everything happens for a reason, or blaming the moon or the mercury retrograde instead of working through and feeling your true emotions. Spiritual practices are so important and can be extremely helpful in hard times, but automatically trying to see the blessing in everything without processing your emotions doesn't allow you to accept and acknowledge the truth. I believe we are souls having a human experience and we need to see both sides. Sometimes that means asking ourselves if we are using our spirituality to bypass our emotions instead of accepting and working through them. Yes, if you are an empathic person, you can't deny that you are affected by the moon and other people's energy, but you can't blame all your thoughts and feelings on those influences. You have to be willing to take ownership of what is yours to deal with and leave behind what's not. Your power lies in knowing the difference.

The Next Big Shiny Object: This suppression style is very common among high achievers, because we are so easily distracted by excitement! Most of the time we don't even realize we are doing it. I am definitely guilty of attempting to replace the pain from one thing with the pleasure of another. For me, this looked like me jumping into the next big project or goal when something in my life became difficult. It was my way of keeping busy enough to distract myself from the pain I was feeling, but ultimately always led to more pain and frustration because I was never finishing my goals or dealing with my problems head on. I am a sucker for being distracted by shiny new things and the feeling of excitement I get from diving into something new and challenging. For some, this suppression style looks like retail therapy. Buying the new car, new house, or new wardrobe in attempt to distract yourself and feel good in the moment. Who doesn't love a little retail therapy!? For others, this may be jumping into a new relationship which can feel exciting and fun at first but doesn't actually fix the underlying emotional issues that you have yet to work on. This is why you attract partners with similar personalities and repeat relationship problems until you break the cycle by facing and healing the issues inside yourself.

Being Super Woman: This is for you, Miss Independent. You are the driven, goal oriented, successful, self-sufficient, alpha type who thrives on being strong and in control. You tell yourself to push through, persevere, and to be strong when things get tough. You don't give yourself permission to feel or be in the moment. You may look strong on the outside, but you are falling apart on the inside and trying to keep it together. You are amazing at giving yourself a pep talk and carrying on as you ignore your own feelings. Your feelings *are* worthy of your time and attention, and it is okay to be vulnerable. Having emotions isn't a weakness, but not being able to deal with them is. Vulnerability is necessary for healing and processing. Being harsh on yourself and using your strength as your way of suppressing may improve your performance temporarily, but in the long run it is a recipe for burnout and resentment. True emotional strength comes from the awareness of knowing when you need to be strong vs when you need to take some time to reflect on your emotions, so you can learn and grow from them.

I am guilty of all of these! Having awareness that you are suppressing is the first step in making a change. Give yourself some grace and maybe some tough love, too. Chances are, you learned how to handle your emotions from your parents or those you were close to growing up. Think about how your parents handled stress and anger. Did they react strongly by screaming or yelling, or did they get quiet and disappear? We tend to pick up their ways even if we hate to admit it. Your season of life will change, potentially causing your suppression style to change with it. Now that you are aware of your suppression style, it's up to you to commit to not relying on it during emotional times. Next time you are feeling strong emotions, don't try and stop them. Instead, ask yourself *why* you are feeling the way you are. The willingness to dive in deep may reveal some harsh truths about some things you need to change, but that is the beauty of living and learning.

What can you commit to doing differently next time you feel the urge to suppress your emotions? Journal? Talk it out? Beat the crap out of a pillow? Throw an adult tantrum? Cry? Processing thoughts and emotions looks different for everyone. My go-to ways of processing are journaling and talking it out. What I can't work out in my mind through journaling, I talk through with someone I love and trust. Sometimes this means I want their guidance and opinion, and other times I just need them to listen so I can verbally get it out in order to process it and feel better. I can't tell you how many times I asked my husband to just sit and listen while I unload my thoughts and get something off my chest. It feels good to just get it out! Sometimes a good cry feels amazing, too. The point is to *feel*. Give yourself the permission to experience your emotions from start to finish.

Have you ever watched a toddler throw a tantrum? They get mad, then sad. They scream, then cry, then whimper, then they are done and move on. They ride the emotion all the way through without judging themselves or worrying about who might see them or what they might think of them. So, go ahead, lock yourself in your room and throw an adult tantrum! Beat a pillow, scream, cry, and let it out. See how it feels to release those built up emotions. When you are done, you will have diffused some anger and can handle the situation with a calmer mind. I think journaling is a great diffuser too. Before you unload a ton of anger on someone, write down how you are feeling. Let that pen flow freely! This will help you express and release some of your anger before having to confront someone or a situation as an emotional wreck. This will save you a lot of embarrassment and apologies for saying things in the heat of the moment that you didn't mean and can't take back. We have all felt the regret of getting wrapped up in our emotions and saying things we wish we wouldn't have.

Maybe you just aren't the type to speak your mind, so you hold onto your thoughts and bury your emotions deep down. I see this quite a bit when working with clients who feel personally victimized or traumatized by someone. I know it seems impossible to forgive this person for the pain they caused. Forgiveness isn't about forgetting what that jerk did to you; it's about finding peace for yourself. Forgiveness doesn't let that person off the hook or justify what they did. It just means you are ready to release your emotional attachment to it by cutting the energetic ties that other person holds on you. So, how do you actually forgive someone when it seems impossible? You connect with what happened, and allow yourself to go there and embrace it fully without suppressing the attached emotions. Journal on it. Meditate on it. Verbalize it to someone you trust. Forgiveness is a choice. Does it happen overnight? Heck no! It shouldn't, because it takes time to process feelings and recover from emotional damage. I know it can feel near impossible to move forward from it, but freeing up that energetic space takes away any control that person has over you. Quit giving them your precious energy and power, because they don't deserve it; you do.

It's also important to forgive yourself as well for any responsibility you hold in the situation. Maybe you stayed too long in a relationship you knew was all wrong, or you ignored the warning signs telling you to cut ties with someone or you enabled the other person in some way. I'm not saying you should blame yourself, I *am* saying you should forgive yourself for any part you had in it and decide to take it as a lesson that you can learn from and not repeat. A really powerful exercise you can do to help you forgive and release any anger you still have for that person is to write them a letter they will never see. I like to burn the letter after I write it to represent me letting it go. The intention of this exercise to release your anger so you can move on. This doesn't mean you forget what happened, this means you are telling the universe you are ready to rid yourself of the toxic emotions you associate with it. You can do this anytime, but a full moon is the perfect time to purge emotional energy that is no longer serving you. Light a candle, write your letter, and watch it burn in the moonlight. It's so freeing!

Some of the most common letters are:

1. Heartbreak/Divorce/Break-Up Letter

Use this for any breakup from your past that has left an emotional residue and may be blocking you from being fully happy in your current or future relationships. It may look something like this:

> Dear so and so,
> I am sad because…
> I am angry because…
> You made me feel…
> You broke my heart because…
> I think you are an a** because…
> I wish you would have…
> I wish I would have…
> You taught me that…

2. Screw You/You Suck Letter

Call it whatever you want. You are pissed off and it's time to give that person a piece of your mind. Use this for the person who hurt you, betrayed you, used you, stole from you, dumped you, lied to you etc. It may look something like this:

> Dear so and so,
> F-You because…
> I'm hurt because…
> I am angry because…
> I am ashamed because…
> I can't believe you…
> What did you do…
> I am embarrassed because…
> What I wish you would have done…
> What I really want from you is…
> You taught me that…

3. Parent Letter

Unresolved issues with your parents? Who doesn't?! They are human, too, and did the best they could based on what they were taught. You may have taken something they did or said and attached a belief to it that resulted in pain, anger, or a limiting belief that you have carried with you into adulthood. It can be helpful to write your parents a letter to bring to light any unresolved issues you are holding onto. It may look something like this:

Dear Mom/Dad,
When I think of you, I feel…
Wish you would have…
I am disappointed in our relationship because…
What I want most from you is…
I want you to know…
I loved when you…
Thank you for…
You taught me that…

I highly recommend finishing your letters with what you learned from this person. This puts a positive spin on a negative issue. There is something to learn in every situation and if you choose to grow from it, you are winning.

Do I want you to feel your emotions? Yes! Does this mean indulging in them to the point of letting them hold you back and keep you stuck? Heck no. Becoming emotionally free means understanding why the emotion is there in the first place. Learning to process will make you feel energetically lighter and free up space to receive more abundance, peace, and calm into your life. Being emotionally free also means less anxiety. Deep emotional work can be very difficult especially when working through trauma. I highly recommend seeing a counselor or therapist if you see a potential danger in working through or reliving traumatic events. There is no shame in getting the extra help you need!

I have also found reiki healing to be hugely helpful for my clients in times of emotional healing. Reiki is a Japanese spiritual energy healing technique that promotes healing and is amazing for stress reduction and relaxation. I practice Reiki on my clients as an additive therapy to help them as they work through the difficult feelings that come with unpacking heavy emotional baggage.

One of the most rewarding parts about coaching clients is watching them transform and use their personal struggle to help others overcome theirs. So much healing can come from courageously sharing your truth. I think it is hard for high achievers to be open about their struggles because vulnerability can sometimes feel like a weakness. Your willingness to share is inspiring and appreciated by those who need your message. The most beautiful unexpected connections happen when you are open, honest, and raw with your truth. That is the reason I wrote this book, to share my struggles and connect with people who can relate to my stories. Sharing can be scary, but I always remind myself that someone needs me to be brave. My mess is my message. Someone needs you to be brave, too.

Chapter 8
The Limit—Perfectionism

I have way more ladyballs than I do brains. Yep, I said ladyballs. I truly believe every successful high achiever has more balls than brains. Why? Because they take risks in spite of their fear of failure. They jump in and take action and spend more time doing than planning. I believe entrepreneurs definitely fall into this category. The success rate for new businesses is super low. You have to be crazy to invest your time, money, and reputation not knowing if you will succeed... and crazy is exactly what it takes. Entrepreneurs are some of my favorite clients to work with, because they know their time and energy is super valuable, so they take action because they don't have time to waste. They *are* their business, so taking care of and investing in themselves means better productivity *and* a thriving business. They are resilient and know better than anyone that failure is inevitable, and that success is built on failures not wins.

Take a look around. Your car, computer, fridge, toilet, favorite TV shows, the music you listen to, the roads you drive on, the company you work for, that podcast you love, the shoes you wear, the Starbucks you drink, the hair products you love, *this book you're reading*…everything you use daily was invented by someone who decided the risk was worth the potential reward. They failed over and over again, but decided to learn from their failed attempts and kept trying. They didn't play it safe and they didn't give up when someone told them they couldn't do it. It took some major faith, confidence, hard work, and *balls*. Not everyone is willing to take big risks in life. Not everyone is willing to stay the course when it becomes difficult.

My point? Stop waiting until the right time to go for it. That goal you want so badly, that business you want to start, that leap of faith you haven't made yet, there will never be a right time and things will never be perfect when you start. Don't let that fear stop you. Be that imperfectly bold and daring woman who is willing to stand out in order to step into her greatness. So often, high achievers are perfectionists because they are wired to want to do things to the best of their abilities and produce good quality work. Perfectionists do great work, but they can easily be held back or slowed down by their desire to make everything perfect. It's an exhausting internal battle that is so easy to get wrapped up in.

How many times have you not gotten past the initial planning stages of something great because you didn't have everything mapped out perfectly and you were afraid to fail? Perfectionism is a great way to procrastinate. On the flip side of that, perfectionism can also make you think you can do it all so you end up overcommitting. Overachievers are notorious for taking on too much and spreading themselves too thin because they won't let anyone help them. Delegating can feel scary, because it feels like you're handing over your power and control. We live in the mentality of "if you want something done right, do it yourself." We assume someone won't be able to do something as good as we do, and if we are totally honest with ourselves…we want the credit and praise that comes from doing it ourselves. You will never reach the level of success you desire if you aren't willing to let go of some control, drop the perfectionism, and start before you are ready.

Perfectionism and procrastination kill dreams. I used to be amazing at using my to-do list as a way to procrastinate. I filled that to-do list with so much nonsense. I would write in normal everyday life tasks like shower, wash laundry, clean floor, do dishes, and make dinner. I lived for that feeling of marking things off my list. It made me feel accomplished and organized. I would even add things in I already did that day just so I could mark them off. Everything I got to mark off felt like a little victory, but it honestly got so ridiculous. I would spend more time stressing over organizing my day then I wouldn't accomplish anything. I even went as far as joining a to-do list loving Facebook group… yes, they exist. It was a group filled with women who love to decorate their calendar and they spent more time decorating it than doing any of the tasks in it. I am all for a pretty calendar, but these women took it to a whole new level.

Obsessively organizing my busy work satisfied my anxious need to distract myself, but it didn't take me long to realize I needed to leave that Facebook group and actually *do* something. I kept telling myself that when I finish this and that, then I can sit down to work on my dreams. Well, that time never comes because that dreaded to-do list never ends. There will always be laundry to do, dishes to clean, and floors to mop, so you must stop using busy work as an excuse to keep you from things that really matter: your dreams, your life purpose, and spending quality time with your family. Anxiety has a way of keeping you busy, but busy doesn't always mean productive. You know the busy types who can't sit still for too long because they start to feel uneasy if they aren't doing something? This was me. The thought of relaxing brought me instant guilt, so I was always doing something, usually more than one thing at a time. I became so frantic and unfocused that every action was a result of multitasking and admittedly it was usually half-assed. I used to pride myself on multitasking because it made me feel efficient. The opposite was actually true. Multitasking kept me from doing anything well. *Multitasking is a lie.* I wasted more time from having to go back to finish things that I hadn't completed because I only gave partial attention to them to begin with.

Next time you are too busy to work on your goals, ask yourself if you have created busy work as an excuse to procrastinate because you are fearful. High achievers are efficient with their time and accomplish tasks by putting one foot in front of the other. They don't always know how they will get something done; they just know they will make it happen. Taking action on your dream can be scary, but I have found that fear makes an amazing roadmap in life. High achievers find success because they chase their fears. They don't allow themselves to stay stuck in their comfort zone for long. Comfort brings stagnancy and stagnancy brings anxiety. Taking action and following your fears creates momentum. The universe rewards action. Messy action. *Real* action. The action that makes you want to barf and crap your pants. The action that feels like a risk, not the busy work that you have to do to sustain yourself and your family. On the other side of your fear is the good stuff, the reward, the confidence.

I know you might be thinking, "But I *am* busy! I have a family to take care of and a job and, and, and…" I get it. Join the club. Everyone *thinks* they are busy. I have a long-time friend who we will call Joe. Joe is an unmarried guy with a full-time job, a house, a girlfriend, no pets, and a car. Joe and I have had many conversations about his life goals and what he wants to accomplish. I have heard everything from having a food truck, to fixing and flipping homes, to designing shirts, to making pickles. He began working on his ideas a few times, but the excitement eventually always fizzled out. I always loved hearing his progress, and then all of a sudden he would just stop talking about it. It made me so sad, because he was so talented and smart, but he gave up on his dreams too easily. I would always hesitate to ask him about his progress, because he would get defensive and start spitting excuses, convincing himself that it will never work or it's the wrong time or….

One day I saw that his excitement for his latest project was gone and his light was dimmed, so I nonchalantly said, "Hey, Joe, there are a couple books I have read lately that I think you will love." These were motivational books I had read that got me pumped up and inspired to tackle my dreams.

He rolled his eyes and said, "Yeah they are probably the same books my sister suggested I read. She said they would change my life."

"So, are you going to read them?" I asked.

Joe laughed and shook his head. "Like I need anything else on my plate right now. I am too busy to read!" he said, with an irritated look on his face as if he was slightly offended.

"Oh, you could get the audio book. I rarely read either. I listen in the car or while I am getting stuff done around the house," I replied.

"I don't have time for that," he said.

I looked at him, confused. *He* is too busy? He couldn't be serious. I was immediately annoyed and wanted to strangle him as I pictured his life of ease with minimum responsibilities. I let it go and didn't even mention the book titles, because I could tell the conversation wasn't going anywhere good. He had his mind made up, and I knew that I wanted something for him far more than he wanted it for himself. Why couldn't he see his wasted potential and endless made up excuses? He *does* have time to work on his dream. He is one of the most creative and artistic people I know who has such great potential, but he keeps giving up. I know he wishes he was doing more. I know he wants to live out his dreams.

So, what's stopping him?

He is.

Inaction has turned into stagnancy. Fear of failure and lack of vision are keeping him stuck. It is frustrating to watch such wasted talent and time, but he has to decide and want it for himself. No one finds success with waiting. Circumstances will never be perfect. It will never be the *right* time. You have to be willing to go for it. I am a firm believer in how you do one thing is how you do everything. So, if you are someone who struggles to finish things, chances are you tend to quit on most things in life. If you are making excuses about cooking dinner or going to the gym, it's probably safe to say you are really good at making excuses for other things in your life. People who have a hard time taking ownership for their life tend to be really good at blaming other people or circumstances for everything. *How you do one thing is how you do everything.* Think about that. No one is perfect but having the awareness of your patterns and excuses can be so powerful. Awareness is necessary for you to be able to call yourself out when you are "doing that thing again" or using that same excuse or quitting on yourself yet again. Stop thinking you aren't good enough for your goals. Stop thinking you don't have what it takes to accomplish what you want. Your excuses suck, and they simply aren't true. The reality is, if you want something badly enough, you will make the time to do it, period. Get up. Make the time. Do the darn thing. Fail. Go at it again. Do it for you.

Grab your journal and ask yourself the following:

- What am I putting off that I want to do but am fearful of?
- What goal have I given up on?
- What busy work is keeping me from my big dreams and goals?
- What tasks could I start delegating to others to free up some time?
- Am I doing too many things at once?
- What excuse have I been making?
- What needs my attention most right now?
- What would feel really good to accomplish today?

- What are three things I can do today to push me closer to my goal?
- How can I push out of my comfort zone today?

In order to hold myself accountable to my dreams, I had to start using my calendar and to-do list as an effective tool to improve my productivity and efficiency instead of allowing it to become an anxiety producing excuse to procrastinate. I found myself making multiple lists all day long. I would write them, rewrite them, then add to them and next thing I knew I would have four lists written in one day and hadn't accomplished a single thing. I finally found a method that works and I credit this method as the reason I maintain my sanity as a productive and busy mom.

Once a week, usually on Sunday, I brain dump a master list of everything that needs to get done or requires my attention. Then every morning, I pick three things from that list and write them on my calendar as my to-dos for that day. Three things moves the needle, and I feel accomplished without feeling overloaded, stressed, and burnt out. Some days I will do more, some less, but knowing I have a running list of things to do relieves stress because I feel organized and able to prioritize.

I recommend taking a good, healthy brain dump whenever you feel overwhelmed or stressed about what needs to get done. I find so much anxiety relief just by getting it out and onto paper. I started prioritizing and stopped putting nonexistent deadlines on myself and creating a lot of unnecessary stress. Not everything must get done in one day. I can be realistic about what I can accomplish without feeling like a failure when I can't get it all done *all* the time. It's about having a balance: giving yourself some grace yet holding yourself accountable. That beautiful balance is how things get accomplished and goals get met with less anxiety.

Chapter 9

The Limit—I Am Not My Priority

There I was in that paper-thin gown sitting on the O.B.G.Y.N. table waiting for my doctor to come in for my yearly exam. Ladies, you know the feeling. It's a mixture of awkward, annoying, and "let's just get this done as quick as physically possible before I sweat through this gown." As I sat there nervously tapping my fingers on my legs, I glanced down and oh my gawd what the, is that my leg hair?! I didn't even know it could get that long! I'm pretty sure I could have braided it if I tried. I tried smoothing it down, as if it would actually help, and my legs were so dry and ashy, my skin just flaked off as I watched it fall to the floor. Geez, Kelly, ever heard of lotion or a razor? The doctor is going to think it snowed in here. Just when I thought the leg hair situation was embarrassing enough, I caught a glance of my toenails. Holy half-painted talons! What had happened to me? I could have literally injured myself or someone else with those things. I thought my shoes felt tighter lately.

I jumped off the table nervously and paced the room. Okay, Kelly, get a grip, I tried telling myself. The doctor won't even notice, but if she does, guaranteed she has seen far worse, right? You're here so she can look at your downstairs. Speaking of, I glance down as I lift up my robe…wow, and I thought my legs were bad. I didn't know who to feel worse for, my husband or her. I was so embarrassed and disappointed in myself. Not because I let my body hair grow too long or because I had not painted or cut my toe nails in forever, but because I wasn't taking care of me like I should.

Let's be honest, this wasn't the first time I had gone awhile without shaving my legs because, duh, *winter*. It wasn't that big of a deal really, but for me it went beyond grooming. I was letting myself go. I had gained weight and I was not working out regularly. I had not gotten a pedicure in almost three years, my eyebrows were a disgrace, and I couldn't remember the last time I relaxed in the bath, got a massage, or just sat down to watch some trashy reality TV. I have to be fully transparent. My anxiety makes it so easy to go, go, go and constantly do, do, do, but really hard to slow down and take care of myself. Admittedly, I am still a work in progress in the self-care department. I know just how important it is to take care of my mental, physical, and spiritual bodies in order to live my best life but…kids, bills, chores, real life. Balance is nearly impossible when you are in a chaotic season of life, and sometimes surviving is just the best you can do. I could always do better, too, work out more, eat healthier, meditate more, read more, shave my legs more, but I am choosing to give myself grace because I am momming *real hard* these days. I've got the van and an emergency supply of dry shampoo, baby wipes, and caffeine to prove it. I try and focus on what matters most and take it one day at a time. I know it is easy to feel pulled in a million directions when you want to do all the things, and be everything to everyone, but it's not realistic. If you and your kids survived the day and you didn't end up in a straight-jacket in a mental health hospital, be proud of yourself. All joking aside, self-care is the key to your vibrancy and productivity, so let's talk about it.

Masculine and Feminine Energies

If you suffer from high functioning anxiety, just the thought of taking time for yourself and slowing down can feel stressful. Because if you slow down, nothing gets done! I get it. Self-care doesn't have to be something that stresses you out, takes up a lot of time, or disrupts your productivity. If you are feeling resistant to the idea of taking time for yourself for fear of wasting time, you are in the masculine energy of doing, achieving, pushing, and hustling. *This was me.* Always *doing* and never just *being*. I thought that success required a ton of hustle and always being *on*. I watched my parents hustle and work hard for their money and it was engrained in my beliefs that hard work was the only way to earn and be successful. So, I mirrored my beliefs and took my work ethic to the extreme. I was Miss Independent who was freshly divorced, carrying a ton of financial responsibility with the dream of living debt free. My stress and anxiety crept in, and I thought the answer was to work even harder. So, I picked up more shifts and started a side hustle. Work was always the answer to my emotional ups and downs. Stressed about money? Work more. Worried about your future? Start a side hustle. Worried about finding love again? Workout. Tired? Too bad. Get going. Stop wasting time.

My work ethic was fear-based and that didn't feel good, even when I did reach lofty goals. I was so stuck in the masculine energy of action that I never gave myself a break. It never occurred to me that I was lacking the beautiful feminine energy of slowing down and taking care of my mind, body, and soul. No wonder I had anxiety! I knew how to push myself to the point of exhaustion, but I couldn't relax for the life of me. We all possess both masculine and feminine energies that offer a beautiful duality when they are expressed in harmony of one another. Most people tend to be dominant in one energy over another.

The feminine energy is slower, more tuned in, nurturing, and goddess-like. This energy is dominant when doing things like self-care, meditating, yoga, or journaling. In this space, you are creative, intuitive, and able to better receive downloads or guidance from a higher power. The masculine energy is focused, driven, and gets some serious work accomplished. The feminine energy is *being* while the masculine energy is *doing*. You need both because if you stay in only the feminine energy with no action, nothing will get accomplished and if you stay in only the masculine energy with no slowing down, you will get burnt out. High achievers tend to be masculine energy dominant and are really good at reaching goals, but slack on self-care. I spent years in a constant masculine energy pushing and striving and doing just for doing's sake, and I felt completely out of alignment with what I *actually* needed. The beautiful duality of masculine and feminine energies was missing, and I needed to slow down, re-center, and tap into who I needed to be in order to live the life I desired. I will always enjoy working and being productive, but I hated the rushed, chaotic, and frantic feeling that came with hustling *all* the time. I craved more ease, flow, and enjoyment, but honestly felt guilty when I slowed down.

Tapping into my feminine energy feels so refreshing and centering when I do it, but it doesn't come as naturally to me as the masculine energy does. I had to schedule in time to relax, journal, and meditate. Like I literally had to write it on my calendar and make it a "to-do" in order to get it done. I have to remind myself that I need to be a priority over my work and that means taking the time to enjoy myself without feeling guilty. When guilt creeps in, I remind myself how much more productive, creative, and efficient I was when I take time to step away from work and actually *live*.

Energy matters in business too, because it either attracts or repels. The high vibe feminine energy that comes from pleasure is so attractive. It is a receiving energy that also helps to more easily attract clients and abundance. I am able to show up stronger in my business when I take the time to enjoy activities that are feminine energy dominant such as journaling, meditating, enjoying a glass of wine, taking a bath, or vegging out with some trashy reality TV. I can then return to my business feeling more calm, focused, and powerful. It is a game changer. I attract more clients and abundance, making success feel more aligned and less of a struggle.

Taking care of my body was one thing, but everything changed for me when I committed to taking care of my mind. I nourished my mind with personal development podcasts and books, positive affirmations, and positive self-talk. No more calling myself names, running myself into the ground, or beating myself up for making mistakes. The more I turned within and took time to reflect and connect to my feelings, the more answers I found. My confidence grew and my intuition got stronger. I felt more comfortable being myself and started to show up authentically with less concern about what other people thought of me. I felt like I could finally trust myself to take care of my mind and body. It was like I had my own inner B.F.F. I know now how to pull back on the reigns in order to let my feminine goddess energy step up and take over when my ambition gets out of hand.

Boundaries

When I first began my coaching business, I wasn't confident about my message. I didn't really know exactly what I was offering or who I wanted to serve. I just knew I wanted to help people get healthier. I was getting a lot of referrals which felt amazing, but my lack of clarity and unfocused intention attracted people of all ages with many different problems, needs, and goals. I had clients who wanted to lose weight, lose their man, overcome A.D.H.D., recover from stroke, and move on after rape. Some clients were super needy and loved living in Victimland, while others followed all my advice and made coaching effortless and fun. Some, I just didn't vibe with and because our energy didn't align, our sessions felt like a struggle. I knew if I didn't get intentional about who I wanted to serve, I would get burnt out quickly, even though I hated the thought of turning some clients away. I needed to put some intention into my practice and learn how to have boundaries.

When I began coaching and putting myself and my message out on social media, I wasn't being one hundred percent authentic because I thought being my hippy dippy, spiritual, crystal carrying, natural medicine loving self would ruin my credibility as a pharmacist and make me look unprofessional. It' s not typical for a pharmacist to believe in meditation, manifestation, and natural medicine over pharmaceutical medication. Hiding that part of myself from my clients became exhausting. When I began to show up as the real me with clarity and intention, the universe responded by sending me dream clients. I can now proudly say I work with some of the most amazing ambitious open-minded women who want more out of life and are unapologetic about needing a coach to get to the next level.

I am choosey with my energy in business and in life. I can't serve people who are unwilling to take responsibility for themselves. I choose not to be around people who are constantly negative, catty, or jealous. I refuse to spend time with people who constantly pass judgement on my way of living. Saying no to the wrong clients or negative people means I am saying yes to myself and to the clients who are meant to work with me. That is what having healthy boundaries is all about. High functioning anxiety types tend to fear letting others down. We spread ourselves too thin, put ourselves last, and tend to be very sensitive people. We care what other people think and we want to please everyone. Saying no doesn't make you a jerk, it means you are respectful of your time and energy. If you don't respect your own time and energy, others won't either. This is when you find yourself spread too thin because you are doing everything for everyone else, and you have forgotten to take care of yourself.

Raise Your Vibe

Your vibe is everything. It's the energy you bring and how you show up in this life. It's your gift to the world. Energy is so powerful and carried from person to person, causing a ripple effect. Think about that for a second. Your vibe is *that* significant that it can affect so many people you don't even know or come into contact with. Reminding myself of this makes me remember how it is so important to protect it. I am a sensitive person and pick up on people's emotions and energy all the time. I know when someone feels excited, sad, or uncomfortable, and I want to do everything in my power to make that person feel good. Being an empathic person is an amazing gift yet can feel exhausting at times.

Have you noticed how some people completely deplete you of energy, while others are like an outlet you can plug into to get recharged? Think about the people you love being around the most in your life. Why? They probably make you feel good energetically. My closest friends get the highest vibe Kelly. I feel my best when I'm around people who I have an even energetic exchange with. A relationship is most fulfilling when you feel like your energy is reciprocated. Think about how you feel after being around people who are needy, negative, or judgmental. You feel tired, low vibe, and irritable. Life is an energy exchange and constantly hanging around people who are sucking your energy will leave you feeling exhausted. This was a hard lesson for me to learn.

Beware of the energy vampires who suck the life out of you and leave you feeling drained and angry!

I always know when it's is time for me to withdraw and recharge. I become an irritable jerk to those closest to me. I would compare it to P.M.S. when I am completely aware of my low vibe energy and can't even stand being around myself. I feel so on edge and know that almost anything anyone does or says will set me off. It's a gross feeling, and I know if I don't withdraw, recharge, and get grounded it is inevitable I will do or say something out of anger that I will later regret. It's not pretty. The saying, "You can't pour from an empty cup" is so true. You are not showing up as your best self—Mom, friend, wife, coworker—if your cup is empty. Low vibe energy lowers your productivity and reduces your quality of work, too. Losing productive momentum is a true nightmare to a high achiever who craves accomplishment.

So how do you raise your vibe, fill your cup, and reclaim your power? Take time for yourself. Do what lights you up. What makes you feel calm and connected to your highest self? What recharges your batteries? Do what feels good to you.

My favorite way to recharge is to get grounded in nature, also known as "earthing." Earthing is connecting to the earth's natural surface charge which is scientifically proven to reduce inflammation and stress, improve sleep, and help your body heal. I highly recommend the book *Earthing* by Clinton Over, Stephen Sinatra, and Martin

Zucker if you want to learn more about all the amazing benefits of getting grounded. I am lucky enough to live on acreage where I can step outside and be consumed by the beauty and quiet of nature. My soul craves nature's energy. The stillness and peace allow me to disconnect from my mind and connect to my soul and my higher self. My amazing husband built a mile-long nature trail around our property. I have a couple meditation spots where I sit and take in all my beautiful surroundings and journal the chaos of life away. The sounds, the smells, and the peace of nature refuels me. This is where I feel most connected to a higher power and my intuition. This is where I disconnect from distraction. This is where my creativity is born and where my big ideas are downloaded. This is where I pray. When I am in nature, I am in my truest form.

Get outside, take your shoes off, and connect with the healing power of the earth. Breathe in the beauty around you. We tend to rush through life and forget just how many beautiful miracles surround us on a daily basis. Look at the trees. Listen to the birds. Feel the power of Mother Earth restoring you. Breathe it in. These are the moments life is all about.

Chapter 10

The Limit—Running on Fumes, Not Faith

What if I told you there was no possible way you could screw it up, because you are on the right path and destined for greatness. Well, it's true. You are reading this book for a reason. You were guided here and it's part of your journey. I believe 100 percent that we are co-creating our lives with a higher power. I doesn't matter to me what religion or faith you believe in. What I care about is that you believe in *something*, a higher power of some sort that created you or is guiding you. God, Universe, Angels, Source, Jesus, Buddha…I don't care who it is. There is such power in believing in and being grateful for the guidance you are receiving from your creator.

Why does having faith matter? It is so common for those who struggle with anxiety to also struggle with control. I would know. You may feel the need to control things, and not even realize you are doing it. Are you the type of person who gets irritated when things don't go exactly as planned? Do you plan out an entire vacation itinerary with no room for spontaneity? Do you often get upset when people don't do what you expect them to? Do you have a super strict schedule for house chores, homework, meal planning, etc.? When your typical schedule doesn't go as planned, does it throw off your entire mood and day? I'm not saying you shouldn't plan out things, because I know you are busy and it's not realistic for a high achiever to not be organized or follow a schedule. I *love and rely on* a good paper calendar and a to-do list to keep my chaos organized. What I am saying is that we can't control everything, and that loosening your grip on the expectations and standards you hold for your life is energetically freeing.

Life isn't all about rigid schedules, rushing, goals, and to-do lists. There is a place and time for it, but life is meant to be enjoyed too. When you are so caught up in controlling every detail around you, you aren't enjoying the present moment of just *being*. These moments are passing you by and one day you will realize you rushed through life and didn't fully *live* it. Why do we try to control? Fear. Fear of the what ifs. Fear of delegating a task to someone who may never do it as well as you. Even worse, fear that they may do it even better than you. Fear of not being needed. Fear of losing someone. Fear of getting hurt. We tend to try and control our surroundings when we feel out of control. Control feels like an energetic anchor that keeps you stabilized, so letting go of control can be terrifying, I know. Surrender. Let go of control. Give your worries up to a higher power. Surrender the "unknowns" that cause you fear and leak your energy. Surrender the "how" when you know exactly what you want but don't know how you will make it happen. Worry is wasted energy.

This doesn't mean you don't take responsibility for your actions or put forth effort to the things you can change. Having faith just means understanding you are not ultimately in control of it *all*. Of course you have free will, but you are also co-creating with a higher power. Sometimes you are in the driver's seat and sometimes you need to get your butt in the backseat and shut your mouth so the universe can do its thing. You're human, so there are going to be times when you feel like the universe doesn't have your back. It's these times when you need to trust the most. Believe. Do your part in meeting the universe half way and allowing yourself to be taken care of. Giving up control is one of the hardest things for a high achiever to do. Letting go and relying on faith was so much of a struggle for me that I got a tattoo in white ink on my left wrist that says "believe." Sorry, Mom! It reminds me to surrender my worries and believe in the imperfectly perfect path I am on during this lifetime.

Being controlling translates energetically as being desperate, pushy, and needy. It's easy to feel defeated or upset when things don't go as planned. You have two choices when it comes to dealing with your disappointment. Let it go and choose to be grateful for the potential lesson learned/blessing in disguise or… be upset. Everything is happening *for* you, not *to* you. You can either choose to see the good in a negative situation or let the negativity consume you. Gratitude raises your vibe immediately. When your vibe is high, you are better able to manifest what you desire, and reach a beautiful state of receiving. This isn't about spiritually bypassing everything. You are still a human who has feelings and emotions, so it's not okay to just stand back, throw your hands in the air, and say screw it all, because I am supposed to have faith that everything will be done for me. This is about taking responsibility for your life with the understanding that you can't obsess over controlling *every single detail*. You will drive yourself crazy! Hello, anxiety!

So, let's talk about how exactly you choose faith instead of fear, control, and anxiety.

I find it extremely helpful to journal my way through these times.

I sit down with my journal, and ask myself things like:

1. Why am I feeling badly about what's happening right now?
2. What can I do to change what's happening?
3. If I can't do anything about making the situation better, how can I shift my mindset around it?

4. What I am grateful for right now?
5. How can I see this with love?
6. Am I choosing to control? If so, how can I shift into letting go and surrendering?
7. What would my higher self do in this situation?
8. Is there someone who can help me with this situation or with shifting my mindset around it?
9. Will this matter in three years, three months, or even three days from now?
10. Am I being over dramatic?

Big mindset shifts don't just happen with the snap of a finger. They require some work, commitment, and faith. When we are upset about what we cannot control, we are wasting precious time and energy. It's easy to get mad. It's easy to blame someone or something. It's easy to say, "Screw it, I quit." Choose to put one foot in front of the other and take steps forward, even when you don't want to. Choose to learn lessons from failures. Choose to get back up when life pushes you down. Choose to have faith that it will be okay. Choose to surrender and restore your faith *especially* when things feels too heavy to handle.

Chapter 11

The Limit—The Mask

At one of the lowest points during my first marriage, I sat on the exam table crying and confessing to my doctor that my ex and I were fighting nonstop and that I made the appointment because my ex-husband insisted that, "I needed to go get some help." I wasn't even sure what I needed "help" with, but I did know that I was miserable in my drama-filled toxic relationship and struggled with racing thoughts and constant worry. She very kindly told me it sounded like I was depressed from having so much anxiety and also suggested counseling for my relationship. She handed me a script for the antidepressant Lexapro and sent me on my way three minutes later.

I was confused, embarrassed, and felt more hopeless than ever. Anxiety? Nope, not me, I thought. I am super busy, sometimes irritable, and my relationship isn't great, but that doesn't mean I have anxiety or depression. I dispensed this crap to people every day and now *I* was going to take it? Nope. Not happening, I thought. I was in total denial. I *was* stressed out, struggling with my mood, and really tired of running from my personal issues and my marriage problems. I reluctantly convinced myself that the antidepressant would fix my mood and my relationship.

So, I took it. It was awful. I felt dizzy, nauseous, and I was tired *all* the time. My energy level plummeted, and I felt so *off*. I knew that the side effects would be the worst during the first week and that it takes a couple weeks to see the full effect, so I decided to commit to at least a month. The side effects never got better, I didn't feel any happier or less stressed, and my relationship was still a mess.

Turns out I didn't need a medication; I needed to fix what wasn't working in my life. I only took that medication for a couple of months and felt worse than ever and even more lost. I hated putting toxic medication into my body that made me feel like a zombie. I knew there were no magic pills or quick fixes, but at the time I felt hopeless and just wanted to feel better. Medication felt like the best option in the moment, so I can relate when someone feels at a loss and turns to medication for help. I quickly learned it wasn't for me, and I began exploring natural ways to cope with my anxiety first. I tried everything from books to breathing exercises. It felt great to use these practices to lower my anxiety, but eventually learned that in order to manage my anxiety *for real,* I had to discover the actual cause of it. I am in no way judging your decisions if you decide medication is right for you, but I personally feel more aligned with taking a natural approach. Honestly, when I was at my lowest point, I wasn't looking for natural ways to help myself nor was I interested in working through my emotions.

Don't get me wrong, I 100 percent believe that medication can save lives and can be a great way to help reduce anxiety short term. It can be a lifesaver for someone who experiences regular panic attacks or constantly makes themselves sick with worry. But it is never the answer, it is only a way to cope with your feelings until you are ready for the real work of uncovering why it's happening in the first place. Despite what you have been told, anxiety is *not* just a chemical imbalance. This is just a convenient way for Big Pharma to explain it, so you think taking a medication is the only way to correct it. I believe it is beyond irresponsible for the drug companies or a medical professional to lead people to think a medication is the only option. I also think it is completely irresponsible to not ask more questions and do a little more research before popping a pill. Yes, I understand that you are supposed to be able to trust your doctor, but your doctor is just regurgitating what they have been taught. I would know. I was never taught in pharmacy school that there are alternative natural options to treating mood disorders. I certainly wasn't taught to question what the underlying problem actually is. Taking a natural approach to mental health was not something I became interested in until I personally was affected and wanted answers for myself. All types of anxiety are a result of a combination of chemical, emotional, situational, and spiritual causes. This is why it is so important to take a holistic approach to anxiety and to look at it from all angles. I have yet to help a client with just one cause of anxiety.

Here is just a short list of actual causes of anxiety that I have seen with my clients:

- Gut inflammation
- Antibiotic use
- Vitamin deficiency
- Emotional trauma
- Sleep disorder/lack of sleep
- Stress
- Caffeine
- Breast implant illness
- Medication side effects
- Toxic relationships
- Suppressed emotions
- Sexual trauma
- Diet high in sugars, processed foods, or fried foods
- Gluten sensitivity

- Adrenal fatigue
- Food allergies
- Spiritual attachments
- Undiscovered psychic abilities and spiritual gifts
- Lack of exercise
- Learned behavior from parents
- Mental/physical abuse
- Empathic side effects
- Parental abandonment
- Extreme guilt
- Lack of personal physical and energetic boundaries

Uncovering the real cause of anxiety starts with self-awareness. People tend to seek answers on how to make anxiety go away without first asking themselves the tough question of *why* they feel the way they do. Anxiety is your body's way of communicating with you. If you don't listen to the whispers, your body will eventually have to scream to get your attention. This is why anxiety usually starts with subtle signs such as irritability, tension, and worry that can eventually progress into panic attacks, self-harm, or isolation. Anxiety means something in your life is out of alignment with what you need, and your body is trying to tell you so you can make the necessary change. Start asking, "Why am I feeling this way and how can I work through it?" vs. "What can I take for anxiety to just get rid of it?" The willingness to work through comes from an empowered mindset, self-awareness, and the desire for real change.

Nothing changed for me until I made the decision that I was tired of struggling and no longer wanted to let anxiety hold me back. I was experiencing anxiety as a result of poor gut health, learned behavior, stress, suppressed emotions, and toxic relationships. No medication was going to fix those things. I had to decide that *I* was my problem and *I* was also my solution. It took years of researching natural medicine, practicing coping skills, healing my past traumas, learning boundaries, gaining self-respect, and strengthening my spiritual practice. I could have sped up my healing process if I had a mentor to guide me but looking back, it happened naturally at a slow yet perfect pace. Accepting and owning my anxiety was a huge step for me. Consistent journaling, meditating, exercising, and taking the right vitamins and supplements has allowed me to take my power back. Discovering ways to thrive with it, instead of masking it was my way of taking control of it.

Coping skills are great, but only help you to deal with a problem that is ultimately still there. Taking a holistic approach to a happier mood means looking at all potential causes and not just coping. I often start my client on a vitamin regimen, because deficiency of certain vitamins such as iron, magnesium, calcium, B6, niacin, folic acid, vitamin C, or zinc can result in mood disorders. These vitamins are needed for your body to produce serotonin and dopamine, two of the chemicals that keep you naturally happy. If you are deficient, you are more likely to have anxiety and depression. Good gut health is also crucial, because if your gut is inflamed and unhealthy, you cannot properly absorb these vitamins and nutrients which then contributes to the vicious cycle of deficiency and bad mood. I could write an entire book on the importance of good gut health and high quality vitamin supplementation. The majority of your mood stabilizing chemicals are made in the gut not the brain, so focusing on healing your gut is going to be more beneficial than trying to artificially alter brain chemicals with medication.

I often recommend that my clients start their journey by using specific vitamins and supplements to help them correct any deficiencies and ease their anxiety to allow them more clarity as we go deeper into their emotional and spiritual causes of anxiety. This is where my pharmacy side shines, and I make sure we are choosing the safest most effective regimen based on their goals and potential drug interactions with active medications. With this work, there is never a one size fits all recommendation that I can safely make without first asking some questions, so for safety reasons, I won't be making specific recommendations in this book.

I pride myself on providing personalized solutions for my clients. I have helped countless women get off or stay off anxiety and depression meds and it is *the* most amazing feeling hearing those women tell me how vibrant, alive, and authentic they feel without medication. Their confidence grows, their vibe raises, and they shine brighter creating a beautiful ripple effect of good energy on this planet. Is going med free right for everyone? No. I have worked with clients who want to remain on medication but are looking for coping skills and other natural ways to reduce symptoms of anxiety. You have to decide what is right for you. Before you ever decide that you want to stop taking medication, always tell your doctor so they can recommend how to safely taper off your medications. Never attempt to just stop medication. I have had clients try this prior to working with me, and the withdrawal symptoms can be horrible not to mention dangerous. There are vitamins and supplements that can ease the symptoms of medication withdrawal and make the process a lot easier, so never go at this alone. I also highly recommend making your doctor and family aware of your plans to stop taking your medication. This way they can watch for any signs of danger such as worsening mood, depression, or altered mental status.

I can't end this chapter without addressing the elephant in the room. I realize I am a pharmacist promoting a holistic natural approach to healthcare, but I honestly believe that all types of healthcare have their place. I personally have used Eastern medicine, Western medicine, Preventative Care, Natural Medicine, Functional Medicine, Chiropractic Care, Acupuncture, Energy Healing, Crystal Healing, and Prayer. I am *not* against medication. I *am* against masking problems and choosing to suffer or place blame. I *am* against Big

Pharma or their bought doctors leading you to believe you have no other choice besides medication. I *am* against you thinking there is something wrong with you. I *am* against you giving up before you even try to commit to positive change. I *am* all about empowerment and educating myself and others on the best ways *for them* to manage and improve *their* mindset. This looks different for everyone.

I am not here to tell you how to live your life. I am here to tell you that you are in control and have to take responsibility for seeking out the best ways for you to live a happier life. I want you to wake up and stop allowing people, Big Pharma, or whomever influence your decisions about what is best for you. Be your own advocate and just your intuition. If you need help, go get it. Stop wasting time being miserable. Life is too good and too short to live anything other than your best life.

Chapter 12

The Limit—You're a Mean Girl...To Yourself

What if other people were impressed by how well you take care of yourself? What if success by society's standards meant having amazing boundaries, beautifully balanced masculine and feminine energies, and a deep spiritual connection? What if people could visibly *see* the anxiety you feel from the pressure you put on yourself? What if your level of happiness was worn on your sleeve for all to judge? Would you be paying more attention to your mindset then? Probably. But the truth is, we hide our insecurities, anxiety, and stress because it's *not* cute. We don't want other people to see us sweat because we don't want to look weak. We want our ambition and success to be praised and looked up to by others because it feels good. Why are we so concerned about what others think of us when we aren't even giving them the full view anyways? In most cases, "they" aren't seeing the sacrifices, countless failures, or the mistakes made. They aren't with you as you stay awake at night stressing over your endless lists of to-dos. They don't see the pressure that high achievers put on themselves. They don't know what's going on upstairs. All they see is the highlight reel, and that's not real.

If your success is based on fear or pleasing or impressing others, it won't feel good for long. You can't sustain it because there is no passion or fulfillment that comes from living a life according to someone else's standards. Their definition of success is different from yours. Your journey is your own and has nothing to do with other people. No one will care about your dreams or your happiness as much as you do, so you have got to stop thinking about what *they* think and start asking yourself what *you* want. I find that so many people seek out personal development when they are at a crossroads. Maybe you want change or feel change coming on, and it's time to make a shift in your mindset to launch you into the next phase of your life. Chances are if you are reading this book, you have no problem with showing up daily to work on your goals, but I want you to ask yourself if you feel purposeful and passionate about what you are trying to achieve. Does it light a fire in your belly every day? Does it feel like your soul's purpose? Or does it feel heavy and forced? If you are feeling trapped in something you created, it is never too late to make a shift into something that brings you more fulfillment, or in the very least less stress.

Before graduating from the Institute for Integrative Nutrition, I had a side hustle as a fitness coach. I loved fitness because of the positive effect it had on my mood, so naturally, I started helping my friends by holding them accountable to their workouts and meal prepping. I built a community online and even held group workouts in my home. I loved the results my clients were getting, but noticed that no matter what size they achieved, they still were unhappy. I heard a lot of, "When I get back to whatever size, I'll be happy," or "When I lose a certain amount of weight, I'll be happy again." It was never really about the weight or the size. It was about their confidence and not feeling like they were enough. No amount of weight loss was going to fix their limiting beliefs or toxic emotional baggage they were carrying. What they needed was mindset work, not another meal plan or health shake.

I got to the point of dreading talking about the scale, and if I had to talk clean eating one more day, I might puke. I knew I was losing passion for fitness coaching, but felt like I was giving up on my clients or failing if I stopped because I had only been doing it a couple years, and knew they relied on me. I no longer felt aligned in that work, and it became very draining because I knew fitness wasn't the real problem. I wanted so badly to shift into the personal development space, but I was terrified. I mean, *who am I* to feel like I can give advice or guidance on mindset? The fear gremlins crept in. I let my fears take over and paralyze me for several months. I knew it was time to take my own advice and shift into what felt authentic to me: mindset and anxiety coaching. I had been the person who felt consumed by anxiety, and I knew I could help others, but this meant I had to step out and be seen as someone who suffered with anxiety. The vulnerability was almost too much to handle.

I can still remember exactly how I felt as I made the announcement on my social media that I was transitioning from fitness into mindset work. My hands were sweating as I hit the post button on Facebook. I immediately put my phone away and didn't check it for hours. I was afraid of judgement. I was afraid to let anyone down. Mostly, I was afraid of failure. I felt raw and weak. Turns out, it was beautifully received. I had to be true to myself, even if that meant quitting something I had worked hard to build.

High achievers hate to quit. We hate to fail. But sometimes, by not quitting on something, you are quitting on yourself and your dream. It really is okay to shift your focus in order to do what feels exciting and aligned for you. The stagnancy of just going through the motions of something that doesn't feel passionate to you can create anxiety. Stop quitting on *you*. Start showing up every day with true intention for your life. Stop staying in the comfortable familiar place that isn't allowing you to be who you are really meant to be! I'm not saying quit your job tomorrow to pursue your soul's work, because you have to be smart about it. I am a big believer in using your day job to fund building your dream. It can feel frustrating at times to feel in limbo between the two, but I challenge you to choose gratitude instead. Be grateful for the stability of your current position because it is allowing you to work towards something that lights you up.

Pursuing a life of passion usually requires risk and outside-the-box thinking. So many people can't relate to the desire to do more with their life. You are not that person. It is common however, for highly ambitious people to bounce from one idea to the next without fully following through on things. I know it can be so easy to get bored, lose focus, and go towards the next big shiny object. If you do this, you need to ask yourself if you are truly losing passion for what you are working towards, or if you are sabotaging your goals because of fear or anxiety.

I promise that your dreams will be tested. You will have naysayers tell you your idea won't work. People will judge you. People won't understand you. They won't share your vision. It can feel like you are alone, and that no one understands or supports your dreams. Those are normal feelings for a high achiever. We aren't meant to share the same visions or dreams. Just because they don't understand your dream, doesn't make it less valid. It's not their dream! It's yours, so claim it with confidence. It's easy to get all up in your head and give up on yourself. This is why making a commitment to your dreams and personal development is so incredibly important.

The mindset work can be hard, but it's worth it. Once I realized I was my biggest challenge and hardest critic, everything changed. Once I got out of my own way, the flood gates opened, and everything aligned because I was carrying out my calling. My calling and my passion might change, and when it does, it will be okay to make that shift. You aren't stuck doing something unless you keep yourself stuck. We are allowed to shift, change, grow, and do something different. In fact, if you aren't, then you are probably just floating through life and feeling stagnant and bored. How do you make a shift into a life that feels amazing and intentional? You have to be willing to hold yourself accountable to your dreams. You have to be willing to get uncomfortable and take risks that are scary. You have to be willing to admit to yourself and to others what you want out of life without letting their opinions stop you. You don't need anyone's permission. You must allow you, your highest self, and your higher power to be your guide. Screw the naysayers who are doing nothing about their own dreams!

Chapter 13

The Limit—I'm Cured

did all the research. I took all the supplements. I did the self-care. I read the books. I did the meditations. I journaled like a pro. I learned all the coping skills. I did all the things to help my anxiety. I felt amazing. I was happier than ever. I was cured!

Yeah, right.

Do I think you can cure anxiety and never experience it again? No. I think anxiety is meant to be there. I choose to see it as my internal guidance system. When I feel it, I know I need to do some self-reflection and make some changes. You should expect to feel anxiety from time to time. I will be the first to admit that anxiety can make me a real irritable jerk. Moms, I know you share and relate to the dreaded before school morning routine. We are late! Hurry up! Let's go! Put on your freaking shoes! Seriously, Mommy has got to go! I have asked you ten times! Moms, you know the drill. It's miserable and stressful, and it makes me feel terrible for rushing and hollering at my kids when they don't understand why I am so upset and frantic. My energy is so bad when I am feeling rushed, and I know they feel that too, and I hate that.

Yes, kids somehow turn into sloths who forget how to get dressed and put on shoes in the morning, but I had to learn to take partial responsibility. I was sleeping in until the very last second. I pushed snooze at least four times. I was late. I was the majority of the problem. I, once again, didn't leave enough time to sit and enjoy breakfast with them. Feeling rushed brings me instant anxiety. What's the anxiety telling me? Slow down. Prepare better. Stop staying up so late. Stop hitting snooze. Get more sleep. Stop creating a rushed environment! My options are to better my situation, or choose to repeat this stressful morning over and over again. What if you chose to see anxiety as a gift? What if its purpose is to help us instead of harm us?

I believe mindset work is some of the hardest work you will ever do. The emotions that get stirred up when you are working on improving yourself can be really difficult. This is why so many people run and hide from the personal development world. Not you, though. You crave the challenge of being the best most productive version of yourself, right?

You want the best of both worlds, success and happiness without the struggle, anxiety, and overwhelm.

I get it. Anxiety still creeps in for me, but I am able to look at it now with a different perspective. It has purpose. It brings messages you have been ignoring. Expect to face anxiety as you level up in life. When I started my business as a coach, it required me to do things I had not done before such as live videos, podcast interviews, public speaking, calls, consultations, photo shoots. I felt totally vulnerable and exposed. I was putting myself out there for judgment and it was so scary! I was a ball of nerves before I did anything new. My stomach would start to get butterflies, I would sweat and shake, my voice would crack, and my legs felt weak. It was my body's way of communicating to me. I realized that I had the choice of letting the anxiety take over and paralyze me in fear, or choose to see this as an excited energy that I could channel into good. I found it so incredibly helpful to remind myself that I was just excited! Yes, of course I was a little nervous, but mainly I was so excited for the new experience, and it is always helpful for me to remember that anxiety can feel the same in the body as excitement. It is just energy that needs to come out. To release some of that extra energy, I jump up and down as I shake out my hands and repeat over and over how lucky I am to be doing this scary and exciting thing. Another coping skill I love and rely on often is four, seven, eight breathing, a technique developed by Dr. Andrew Weil. This breathing technique was designed to flood the body with oxygen and bring the body into a state of deep relaxation. It works great during times of nervousness or anxiety and can even help you to fall asleep. Breathe in through your nose for four seconds, hold your breath for seven seconds, and breathe out through your mouth for eight seconds. Focus on your breath and repeat as many times as needed to feel more relaxed. The best part about this is that it is discreet and no one knows you are trying to calm yourself down. Give it a try. I do this before public speaking or getting on client calls to reset my energy and restore my calmness. It never fails that whatever I was afraid of wasn't near as scary as I was making it out to be. The fear leading up to it was far worse than actually doing the thing.

Successful people aren't fearless; they just have learned how to manage their fear. If you think about it, it is all made up in our minds. We create the fear and we also decide how we are going to let the fear affect us. This is so empowering to me, knowing that I get to be in control. We can let fear hold us back from anything, if we want to. Remember that, just because you haven't done something before, doesn't mean you should ever assume you won't be able to do it. Look at your amazing track record. You do things all the time that you have never done before. Every time you do something for the first time, you learn. Walking, talking, riding a bike, driving a car, your first job, your first relationship, your first kid, the first time you cooked...I could go on and on. Next time you feel fearful about something, ask yourself:

1. Why does this scare me?
2. What is the worst thing that can happen?
3. Will I regret not doing this thing?
4. What would accomplishing this thing feel like?
5. Am I just excited?
6. Am I making this out to be far worse than what it actually is?
7. How am I benefiting from allowing fear to win?
8. Is this fear holding me back from something I really want?

Personal development is a lifelong journey that requires commitment and practice in order to be effective. What are you consuming on a daily basis? What type of energy are you surrounding yourself with? What are you doing to keep your mindset on track? I can promise that you will fall back into old habits, old limiting beliefs, and negative thought patterns. You will forget to take care of yourself and your boundaries will once again suck. It happens. You're human. But now that you are self-aware, you can be resilient and bounce back stronger than ever. This is how I take control of my emotions when I feel consumed and controlled by them.

- Ask myself *why* I feel the way I feel
- Journal it out
- Get grounded
  - I get out into nature. I get my bare feet on the ground or sit against a tree and take in all the good vibes that nature has to offer.
- Talk it out with someone
- Meditate
- Workout
- Self-care
  - A bath, a book, or a binge session of reality TV

I do the work by figuring out what is bothering me and why, then I dive into self-care afterwards if needed. I don't try and suppress it. I don't allow it to consume me and throw me into a downward spiral of emotions.

I acknowledge it.

I work through it.

I control my emotions. My emotions don't control me.

Conclusion

I was living a double life as a pill pusher by day and a natural medicine lover by night. I was a weirdo carrying crystals in my lab coat pockets. I was hiding behind my white coat suffocating in silence about what I *actually* believed to be true about the power of natural medicine and mindset work. They changed my life, and I knew it was my calling to share my truth, yet I was terrified of coming out looking like a walking contradiction. What would people think? What would they say? Would they think I was total quack? Would my parents feel embarrassed by me? They probably wish their daughter would keep her mouth shut, not ruffle any feathers, and just go to work and make a decent living.

They didn't say that, but my inner dialogue can be super dramatic, and I had myself convinced I would be shunned from the family for doing something with my life that went against my education and super important diploma. No matter how much I tried to hide it, I loved mindset work, spirituality, and natural medicine, and it didn't take long before I became a full-on personal development junkie. For years, I read all the books, listened to all the podcasts, and went to all the conferences. I loved the high I got from other people giving me permission to do something big and different with my life. The more I took in, the stronger the itch became to help people drop the meds, the lame excuses, and the fears, and start living a life full of passion and purpose. No more pursuing things because they thought they should. No more living out someone else's dream or expectations. No more living by someone else's rules. No more hiding and pretending to be okay with a life you don't feel lit up about. I was full of passion and fired up, but the problem was that I wasn't actually *doing* anything. I so desperately wanted to have a thriving coaching business, yet I was scared to start because I always needed just one more book to read, one more certification, or one more podcast to listen to that was going to make me *ready*. One more book turned into many, and someday turned into years of waiting.

Clearly because I am writing this book, I really do love and believe in the power of personal development. Seeing other people step out and take big risks in order to live out their purpose gave me the permission and motivation I needed to do great things without worrying about shining too bright or being too much for some people. I want to be that person for you, but all the personal development in the world is never going to make you ready. If you aren't actually doing anything with the motivation, then what is the purpose? It felt like I was one of those people who went to church consistently and felt amazing while I was there, but then when I left, I acted like a sinner who never sat through a church service. I was basically using personal development as another way to numb out and feel good, but in reality it was becoming a distraction. I was looking for other people to tell me I was good enough. I had many gurus I followed and listened to while secretly being jealous of what they had created with their lives. I so badly wanted to share the self-improvement space with them, but fear held me back.

I share this, because I had to give myself some tough love and a real kick in the butt. I didn't need to read another book or take another online course, I needed to get out from under my mountain-high pile of personal development books, get out of my own way, and just start! I started to be productive and take action on things that moved the needle instead of using research and learning as an excuse to hide. I had to be my own hero and guru and stop looking to others for all the answers. It was time to stop consuming and start creating and to face what I honestly feared: judgment.

Of course people will judge you. Who cares? Why let other people's opinions hold any weight? Why waste your energy on worrying about someone's opinion when they don't even really give a crap about your dreams? I can guarantee you spend far more energy worrying about them than they do thinking about you. Get out of your own way. Stop using every little worry as a way to keep you stuck. You are the only thing stopping you from living the life you want. Stop blaming others and take ownership right now. Without owning your problems, you have no chance at greatness or happiness, and I can guarantee you playing victim will kill your dreams.

I want this book to be the one that gets you to make the change you most need in your life right now, even if it is scary or uncomfortable. Take the leap, make the change, walk away from the toxic relationship, treat yourself, drop the excuses, start making self-care a priority, stop the negative self-talk, quit lying to yourself, stop letting anxiety win, stop quitting on yourself, and start taking steps toward a future that feels good to you. What do you need most in your life to feel happier and less anxious? Whether that's slowing down or taking action, get really *real* with yourself right now. You are in charge of you.

Don't let this book be just another one that you read and forget about what you learned a few days later. Set your intentions, take action, and do the work, because you are worth the effort and you deserve to enjoy a life that feels in alignment with your goals and happiness. High achievers are my favorite type of person to work with because they are creative visionaries with high expectations of themselves and they are always willing to put in the work. Truth is, sometimes we just need someone to hold us accountable to doing the things we are most resistant to. Those are the things that dreams are made of. What you resist doing is exactly what you need to focus on and be held accountable for. You can make huge shifts if you take this book to heart and do the work, but having a coach who believes in you and holds space for your personal expansion is so incredibly powerful. I believe in you, and no, your dreams are not too big or out of your reach. Remember, you are enough. This is your journey. Your life. Your choice. Make it amazing.

Acknowledgements

Luke, I couldn't ask for a more amazing, kind-hearted, gentle, patient husband. You are my everything. Seriously, what would I do without your constant support and love? You have never questioned my crazy ideas or doubted my abilities for one second. You are the most amazing father to our kids, and I think we make the best team ever. I am so grateful for your ability to see things in a completely different way than I ever could. The comfort I feel from you is priceless. Thank you for being you, and letting me be me. I love you beyond words.

Mia, Ryann, and Lincoln, you are my inspiration. I am so proud of you for all that you are and all that you will become. May you always have the courage to chase your dreams and push past your fears. You amaze me every day, and I am so incredibly blessed and lucky to be your mom. Thank you for choosing me. I love you so, so, so, so, so, so, so, so, so, so much. I will forever have the most so's. Muah!

Jim Rompel, thank you for your nonjudgmental wisdom and unconditional love. You are the catalyst that gave me permission to pursue my dreams. You taught me what faith is all about and continue to help me strengthen my spirituality every day. Thank you for the light you bring to this world. I am forever grateful for your knowledge, calming energy, and huge heart. I love you.

To my mom and dad, thank you for all you have taught me. You helped shape the woman I am today, and for that, I am so grateful. You always saw my potential and would never let me quit when things got hard, even when I thought dance was just too hard at age four…boy, was I wrong. Some of my best memories came from those moments of achieving what I never thought was possible, and I have you to thank for that. Thank you for all you have given me and done for me. Love you.

To Bridget and Nicole, I am so lucky to call you my family. I feel most free to be me when I am with you. Thank you for all the support, inspiration, and dance parties. There is no one I would rather shake my stuff with. May our greasy hips never break and our dance parties never end.

Thank you to my Network Pharmacy family for embracing my weirdness and loving me anyway. We have been through so much together, and I can't thank you enough for all the hilarious stories I will carry with me forever. You make me feel at home even at work. Love you guys!

A huge thank you to Dr. Angela Lauria, without you, I may have never accomplished my dream of making an impact with my message. Thank you for the guidance and high-vibe energy. You truly love what you do, and it shows. To my amazing editor, Moriah Howell—you are the most gentle, kind-hearted, patient soul; thank you for your beautiful editing skills.

To the Morgan James Publishing team: Special thanks to David Hancock, CEO & Founder for believing in me and my message. To my Author Relations Manager, Margo Toulouse, thanks for making the process seamless and easy. Many more thanks to everyone else, but especially Jim Howard, Bethany Marshall, and Nickcole Watkins.

Thank You

Thank you so much for reading. If you are ready to shift out of anxiety and overwhelm, I want to help you get really clear on where to start your journey. One of the most common questions I get is, "How do I figure to what is causing my anxiety?" Don't worry; I got you!

I created a free video to help you uncover what's potentially fueling your anxiety and the next steps to managing it naturally.

Check it out here: www.kellyrompel.com/whyanxiety

Light and Love,

Kelly

About the Author

Kelly Rompel is a pharmacist, mindset empowerment coach, author, and reiki healer. She is the creator of the *Rebel Whitecoat* Podcast and *Limitless*, a program for highly ambitious women who want to lower their stress and anxiety. She specializes in a holistic approach to anxiety relief through natural medicine, mindset work, and coping skills. She has helped countless clients safely get off prescription anxiety medication and manage their anxiety naturally.

After earning her Doctor of Pharmacy degree from St Louis College of Pharmacy in 2006, her love for natural medicine and personal development grew, inspiring her to further her education at The Institute for Integrative Nutrition, where she earned her health coaching certificate in 2016. Her holistic approach to coaching combines pharmacy knowledge with her love for natural medicine, energy healing, and spirituality. She loves empowering women to take control of their mindset, regain their confidence and deepen their spiritual connection. Her personal experience with discovering and managing her high functioning anxiety inspired her to work with clients and create programs to help high achievers find happiness while maintaining their productivity.

Kelly is a nature lover and lives on twenty-four acres in Illinois with her husband Luke, daughters Mia and Ryann, and son Lincoln.

Printed in the USA
CPSIA information can be obtained
at www.ICGtesting.com
JSHW082350140824
68134JS00020B/1997

9 781642 796131